The Second
Arab
Awakening

The Second Arab Awakening
And the Battle for Pluralism

MARWAN MUASHER

Yale UNIVERSITY PRESS
New Haven and London

Copyright © 2014 by Marwan Muasher.
All rights reserved.
This book may not be reproduced, in whole or in part, including illustrations, in any
form (beyond that copying permitted by Sections 107 and 108 of the U.S.
Copyright Law and except by reviewers for the public press),
without written permission from the publishers.

Yale University Press books may be purchased in quantity for educational, business,
or promotional use. For information, please e-mail sales.press@yale.edu
(U.S. office) or sales@yaleup.co.uk (U.K. office).

Set in Minion type by Integrated Publishing Solutions.
Printed in the United States of America.

Library of Congress Cataloging-in-Publication Data

Muasher, Marwan.
The second Arab awakening : and the battle for pluralism / Marwan Muasher.
pages   cm.
Includes bibliographical references and index.
ISBN 978-0-300-18639-0 (hardback)

1. Arab Spring, 2010–   2. Revolutions—Arab countries—History—21st
century.   3. Arab countries—Politics and government—21st century.
4. Pluralism—Arab countries.   I. Title.
JQ1850.A91M827 2014
909'.097492708312—dc23   2013029236

A catalogue record for this book is available from the British Library.

This paper meets the requirements of ANSI/NISO Z39.48–1992
(Permanence of Paper).

10 9 8 7 6 5 4 3 2 1

To the youth of the Arab world
Who revolted, not against their parents,
But on their behalf.

Arise, ye Arabs, and awake!

—Ode by Ibrahim Yazegi
(Reproduced from the epigraph in
George Antonius' book *The Arab Awakening*)

Contents

Note to the Reader

The extraordinary and tragic events in Egypt during the summer of 2013 took place after this book was well into production, but they should not go unremarked. As I write this, two months after President Mohamed Morsi was forcibly removed from office, and during a week in which more than nine hundred civilians were killed, protesters remain camped out in Cairo and the military rulers have declared a state of emergency. It is clear that this summer will be remembered as a historic turning point. What sort of turning point, and how events will unfold from here, no one can say.

But what has happened so far supports one of this book's major arguments: that the Islamist and secular forces in the Arab world, both before and after Arab uprisings, have shown no solid commitment to pluralistic and democratic norms. Each side has denied the right of the other to operate and has often ignored the popular will.

The Islamist forces in Egypt, winners of the presidential and parliamentary elections that took place after Hosni Mubarak was deposed, pushed through a constitution that ignored the will of a large number of Egyptians. The very reason for adopting a constitution is to achieve consensus among the various forces in society, yet this was a majoritarian document that gave little heed to the opposition. Political frustrations and a deteriorating economic situation finally led millions of Egyptians to return to the street, this time demanding an end not to the secular authoritarian regime of Mubarak, but to what they saw as a new Islamist authoritarian regime.

The secular forces, meanwhile, remained in denial. They continued to act as if the elections in Egypt meant nothing, refusing to cooperate with the Islamists, until they finally sided with the armed forces in deposing a democratically elected president. They thus practiced the same power-monopolizing behavior of which they accuse the Islamists. Chances are that any new constitution will this time ignore the will of the large number of Egyptians who support the Islamists, and will end up being another majoritarian document that will not put Egypt on a path toward stability, prosperity, and democracy.

The silver lining is that the street in Egypt has demonstrated that no leader can behave in an autocratic manner without being seriously challenged. The fear that any force will use democracy only as a means to power, and then deny all other parties the right to operate, seems to be abating. Tragically, it is a lesson that is being learned with blood. Hundreds of Egyptians, and thousands of Arabs elsewhere, are paying for it with their lives. In the end, exclusionist policies cannot prevail, and both sides will discover that only inclusion can bring stability. The battle for pluralism has only begun.

Acknowledgments

This book is a natural extension of my 2008 volume, *The Arab Center: The Promise of Moderation* (also published by Yale University Press). In that book I argued that the notion of "moderation" cannot be selectively applied to Arab governments' attitudes toward the peace process between Israel and the Palestinians, but must also be used to assess their performance on the increasingly critical issue of domestic reform. Little did I know that, three years later, the unsustainable status quo I wrote about would translate into an Arab Awakening that has swept the whole region.

I am grateful to Bill Frucht of Yale University Press, who talked me into writing a short book for the general reader that attempts to make sense of the transformational changes taking place in the Arab world, for the many discussions we had, and for his expert editing that brought much clearer focus to the manuscript. I am also grateful to Jeffrey Schier for his editing of the manuscript.

I am indebted to the many people who contributed to this work. I have benefited over the course of my career from several individuals whose friendship I especially value, and whose interactions have helped shape my thinking. Their comments greatly enriched this manuscript. I am grateful in par-

ticular to Ziad Asali, Rania Atalla, Rula Awwad, Kim Ghat-
tas, Mustafa Hamarneh, Rima Khalaf Huneidi, Abdel Karim
Kabariti, Samir Khleif, Merissa Khurma, and my brother, Su-
heil Muasher.

Jessica Mathews and the Carnegie Endowment for International Peace have provided me with a warm home that
gave me a solid anchor and allowed me to develop a compara-
tive and analytical view of the Arab world. I am grateful to the
many people at Carnegie who worked on, or provided comments for, the manuscript: Mokhtar Awad, Aseel Barghuthi,
Alexandra Blackman, Mai El-Sadany, Manar Hassan, Omar
Hossino, Marina Ottaway, Alexandra Siegel, Jocelyn Soly, Tif-
fany Tupper, Fred Wehrey, and Katherine Wilkens. Nehad
Khader, my research assistant, worked tirelessly, running
down critical factual detail and relevant research for the book,
as well as editing the text, and she deserves special thanks. I
am also very grateful to Dave Kampf, director of communications, whose expert hands greatly enhanced the manuscript.
No words can describe my gratitude to Sarah Chayes, who
served as my sounding board, challenging my ideas, bringing
them into more focus—at times even agreeing with me—but
all the while providing careful text editing of the manuscript,
even redrafting some passages. This book would not have been
the same without her.

Two people deserve special thanks: Dalia Mogahed co-
authored part of the chapter on political Islam, providing in-
sightful analysis of Islamist movements based on her polling
work with Gallup. Dalia is one of the few with an expert view
of the attitudes of people in the region. Muhammad Faour
helped me greatly in writing the chapter on education, with
his extensive experience working on education issues in several Arab countries. I am deeply indebted to both of them.

My wife, Lynne, deserves my eternal gratitude for all the support, input, and good sense she provided and continues to provide during both good and difficult times. Our children, Omar and Hana, inject inspiration and drive on a daily basis. They are my pride and joy, my constant reminder that their generation deserves to live in better, more pluralistic societies than those of their parents. It is to them and their generation that I dedicate this book.

The Second
Arab
Awakening

Introduction

Liberal revolutions have come to the Arab world before. Beginning in the mid-nineteenth century, a "first" Arab Awakening took the form of an intellectual revolution in which a number of Arab thinkers started questioning the control of distant Ottoman despots over their nations, and criticizing their own limited contact with the outside world. Their calls for intellectual, economic, and political change laid the groundwork for a new Arab world, eventually resulting in a wave of independence struggles in the 1940s and 1950s.

Ultimately, however, the first Arab Awakening fell short of the aspirations of many of those who inspired it. In the end, colonial autocracies were replaced with domestic ones—often military-backed single parties that took advantage of their revolutionary legitimacy to cement their grip on power. New regimes paid little attention to developing political systems whose checks and balances guaranteed access for all. They saw pluralism as a potential threat.

Unrealized political as well as economic expectations, and the failure to solve the Palestinian issue and provide good governance, marked the postindependence era in the Arab world. For years, the only groups that contended with the ruling elites were those whose organizing principle was religion. Political Islam emerged as the only alternative to one-party rule. Abuses by government personnel, especially the security and intelligence services, and wealth concentrated in the hands of a few kept tensions seething just beneath the surface. Eventually, something had to give. When a Tunisian peddler set himself on fire in December 2010, the second Arab Awakening was launched, taking many by surprise.

The uprisings that breathed new life into the Arab world in 2011 were inevitable, but achieving the protesters' goals is not. That eventual outcome lies in the hands of the people of the countries involved. Outsiders, however, including powerful Western governments, can affect events, but doing so constructively requires clear thinking about events and their root causes. Unfortunately, much Western thinking about the Awakening is mistaken—with the resulting danger that Western action may be misguided. In the brief span of two years, the West lurched from calling this awakening an "Arab Spring"—a name that implied expectations of an immediate transition from autocratic regimes to democratic ones—to seeing it now as some kind of an Arab inferno, because of the rise of Islamic parties with their implicit or perceived threat to liberal democratic advances and their potential flirtation with jihadi violence.

Neither scenario need be permanent or inevitable. And perhaps most important, the profound transformations Arab countries are undergoing will take time. Although some eastern European nations can be said to have sped up the clock after the fall of the Soviet Union, revolutionary political transformation usually takes decades, not years. Western observers and policy makers need to have strategic patience as they follow unfolding events.

The rise of Islamist parties was also to be expected, and should neither surprise nor overly alarm anyone. They alone had the preexisting organizational capabilities required to run nationwide campaigns, and that allowed them to score electoral victories far beyond their level of popular support.

But success in first-ever elections will not necessarily translate into permanent control. Their promise of better governance, which has helped attract support from many Arabs fed up with the status quo, is now being put to the test. As they enter the political fray, this time as decision makers, their perceived "holiness" will be confronted with reality, and their ability to deliver will be established. The question will be whether the constitutional instruments that emerge from the transitional period allow Arab publics—which are conservative but not by and large supporters of theocratic states—to judge Islamists and secular forces alike based on performance, not ideology.

It will take decades to build the foundations of political systems that actually defend democracy and preserve its basic tenets year after year. Some countries will succeed in this process, others will struggle, and yet others will fail. Moreover, it can't be seen through a two- or even a five-year prism; it must take its due course.

Those elements of society that lead the transformation will help determine any country's outcome. The Arab world has long been dominated by two forces—an entrenched, unaccountable elite on the one hand, and Islamists on the other. But neither of these groups—which often have achieved an uneasy modus vivendi—has ever demonstrated a genuine commitment to pluralism.

Third forces are needed. Hope rests with a new generation—the youth who started it all in the streets—that is more committed than its elders to the principles of democracy. So far, this revolutionary young generation has done a better job of defining what it is against than what it is for, and this group will need years to establish the organizational capacity and financial wherewithal to achieve a lasting break from the past.

If it is to succeed where the first Arab Awakening failed, this second Arab Awakening needs to be an assertion of universal values: democracy, pluralism, human rights. These are not ideals that can be imposed upon a region from outside, but they can be encouraged to grow—though it will require patience and an accurate understanding of both the actual conditions and the kinds of actions that are likely to be effective.

In the end, the battle is not solely against the old powers—for new ones may be animated by the same drives. More importantly, it is a battle for pluralism. Only when societies and their elected leaders truly embrace tolerance, diversity, the peaceful rotation of power, and inclusive economic growth can the promise of a new Arab world be realized.

I

Understanding the Awakening

1

The First Arab Awakening
A Battle for Independence

In 1939, an Egyptian Christian of Lebanese origin named George Antonius wrote a book called *The Arab Awakening*.[1] Cambridge-educated, settled in Jerusalem, and personifying so much of the Arab world's religious, cultural, and ethnic diversity, Antonius documented the first liberal era in the modern Arab world. This slowly unfolding phenomenon evolved over the course of a century from an elite intellectual renaissance into grassroots political—and eventually armed—resistance to Ottoman and then Western colonial rule. But the progression dead-ended in the mid-twentieth century. Its initial liberal promise was aborted when foreign despots were replaced by homegrown ones, who went on to rule the region for more than fifty years.

This first Arab Awakening laid the groundwork for the wave of uprisings that first broke out over the region in 2011. Many of the same issues are at stake. Many of the same dangers loom. While the ultimate failure of the First made the second Arab Awakening almost inevitable, that failure also conveys a warning: toppling despotic rulers alone is no guarantee of

a healthy political development. A constructive vision for future polities must be hammered out and must be founded on
an unshakable commitment to pluralism—leading to systems
of protections and inclusiveness that enable what may be the
Arab world's greatest asset: its ethnic, cultural, religious, and
intellectual diversity.

In the early nineteenth century, the predawn of the first
Arab Awakening, what is today considered the Arab world—a
region spanning the Middle East from Iraq through the Levant, the Arabian Peninsula, and North Africa—shared a lin-
guistic, cultural, and religious heritage. Local particularities,
such as remarkably different idioms and even pronunciations,
styles of architecture or traditional clothing, favored economic
activities or schools of jurisprudence, distinguished different
zones. But today's mosaic of nation-states did not exist, nor
was the region a separate political entity, for it had been con-
quered in the sixteenth century by the Istanbul-based Ottoman Empire, which shared the religion of Islam with its Arab
territories, but not the Arabic language.

From its height of power and development in the mid-
sixteenth century, the Ottoman Empire commenced a slow
decline. The Napoleonic invasion of Egypt, from 1798 to 1801,
opened the first crack in the southern flank of this far-flung,
variegated, and largely self-sufficient entity. Those three years
were enough to introduce new, postrevolutionary European
ideas about political organization, science and education, and
administrative reform.

Defeat at the hands of the British forced Napoleon to
withdraw from Egypt, leaving a power vacuum on which an
Albanian commander of the Ottoman troops in Egypt capi-
talized, taking up the title of *wali,* or governor, of Egypt. Many
consider Muhammad Ali to be the founder of the modern

nation. He sent officials to Paris to absorb European ways of thinking and administrative procedures, and he launched numerous reform initiatives.

Thus, this first Arab Awakening can be seen as a movement that began at the top levels of society—among both Arab and non-Arab subjects of the Ottoman Empire—as members of the elite were drawn into a dynamically changing world order, and as they began experimenting with the application of new modes of thought to current problems and traditional learning, and with political and administrative reform within an imperial structure they were not yet challenging. Initially, this awakening was predominantly one of the mind.

A glance at the roster of its most illustrious thinkers demonstrates that many of the countries undergoing transition today were in the vanguard of the first Arab Awakening too. Much of the theoretical work of those men, even the changes they advocated in the physical infrastructure of their provinces, laid the groundwork for a more modern order in their respective countries, and have informed the expectations, aspirations, and demands of today's revolutionaries. Egypt, for example, that intensely vital intellectual and cultural hub, helped lead the way then as now. One of the officials Muhammad Ali sent to Paris was the writer and translator Sheikh Rifa'a Tahtawi (1801–1873). A graduate of one of the most famous institutions of learning in the Islamic world, al-Azhar University, he first studied the French language, and then immersed himself in the thought of the French Enlightenment, poring over the acerbically critical work of Voltaire, Rousseau's theorizing, and Montesquieu's structured compendium on law.

Upon his return to Cairo—passionately proud of its specific history and past glories—Tahtawi began applying European concepts of nationhood within the context of Ottoman Islamic liberalism, seeking justifications for national identity within Islamic thought. More broadly and momentously, he took the first steps toward reopening the door to reasoned interpretation of the sources of Islamic law, the Qur'an and Hadith (sayings of the Prophet Muhammad), which had been considered fixed authorities for centuries. Such interpretation, called *ijtihad,* was seen as near blasphemy at the time. But for Tahtawi, Islamic law could be understood and applied in light of the changing needs of a modern world.

Tunisia, too, whose 2011 uprising inspired a dozen others across the Arab world, supplied its thinkers to the first Arab Awakening. Khayr ad-Din (1822–1890), an Ottoman official of Tunisian origin who rose through the ranks of Ottoman administration to become minister of the navy and eventually the Empire's prime minister, also studied in Paris. In 1860 he helped draft a constitution for Tunisia that, while not yet contesting the fact of Ottoman rule, promoted reform within it, designing some institutional checks on the Turkish ruler's powers over the province of Tunisia.

It is to this mid-nineteenth century period that George Antonius dates what he dubbed the Arab Awakening. He points to the birth of a small literary society, in 1847 in Beirut, whose mission was to promote knowledge and education. From his largely Levantine perspective, Antonius chronicled the activities of several local "enlightened" Arabs whom he saw planting the roots of the movements of national liberation that sought to rid the region of first Ottoman and then Western colonial overlordship in Palestine, Syria, Lebanon, and Iraq. For him, this more narrow nationalistic agenda defined the first Arab Awakening.

Indeed, during the second half of the nineteenth century and the first years of the twentieth, Arabs' willingness to continue living under Ottoman domination began to fray. A combination of the decline of the Empire, and Istanbul's efforts to forestall that decline by redoubling "Turkification" (emphasizing the Turkish element at the expense of other ethnic groups) policies and efforts at centralization, together with the theoretical exploration of nationalist ideas among Arab elites, led to an ideological shift. No longer were these elites calling for reform within the Empire. Increasingly, they demanded a complete break with Istanbul.

In countries with a relatively homogeneous history as separate states—such as Egypt and Tunisia, which boasted their own imperial legacies or admired dynasties—desires for independence from Ottoman rule took on particularist nationalistic overtones. But other thinkers were simultaneously exploring a broader identification, a kind of pan-Arabism, that saw the whole Arab world as sharing a common race, language, and culture. These notions were particularly (though not exclusively) advocated by Christian Arab secularists, especially in the Levant. Their focus was on reframing the modern state around these cultural and historical commonalities, as opposed to around religion. Islam, in their approach, would be incorporated into the overall framework but would not be the defining factor.

Among the secularist intellectuals who developed this line of thought was Butrus al-Bustani (1819–1883), who founded a school in present-day Lebanon that was based on Arab nationalist, rather than religious, principles, and the Lebanese thinker Ibrahim Yazegi (1847–1906), whose ode served as the epigraph of Antonius's book: "Arise, ye Arabs," the first line exhorted, "and awake!"[2]

With the same fervency as that of their Christian neighbors, Muslim Arabs too were among those who promoted these nationalist ideals of political entities that would be independent of Ottoman rule, but whose defining principle would be ethnic—meaning Arabism—rather than religious. Their thinking, too, has nourished that of many present-day revolutionaries.

In their frustration and eventual need for military might to throw off Ottoman rule, some of the early Arab nationalists in the Levant even looked to European powers for help. After all, their forerunners' exposure to European thought, including the importance of the consent of the governed to a healthy and just political system, had inspired their movement in the first place. Little did they realize at the time the trap they were entering.

As the Ottoman Empire was expiring, and even before the First World War hammered the final nail into its coffin, Western powers were jockeying to lay hands on vulnerable parts of it. As early as 1881, the British occupied Egypt. The French looked closer to home, snatching up Tunisia that same year and, by 1912, neighboring Morocco. For its part, Italy had gained control over Libya by 1914. At the end of World War I—and often in violation of promises made to their Arab nationalist proxy forces—Britain and France divided the remaining spoils of the Ottoman Empire. The British Empire gained a mandate over provinces whose boundaries it cut up into modern-day Iraq, Jordan, and Palestine, while France claimed Syria and Lebanon.

As a result of this international grab of land and power, a movement that began as an elite debate over notions of reform within an existing imperial order spread downward and outward to become a grassroots struggle for independence, first aimed at the Ottoman Empire, but rapidly shifting focus to Istanbul's Western successors. The Hashemite dynasty, for example, which ruled the part of today's Saudi Arabia called the Hijaz, launched a popular revolt against Ottoman rule in 1916, fortified by a duplicitous British promise to support an independent Arab kingdom in return for the Arab fighters' efforts against Ottoman forces. Libyans, under the charismatic leadership of Omar Mukhtar, rose up against their Italian overlords almost immediately after Italy took control of their country. And Egyptians, led by such figures as Ahmad Urabi and Sa'ad Zaghloul, fought against the British, gradually gaining independence when the last British soldier left Egyptian soil in 1956—four years after the Egyptian revolution toppled the monarchy in 1952.

For residents of Palestine, the struggle contained an added layer of complexity. In 1917, the British government, through the Balfour Declaration, held out the prospect for Jews anywhere in the world for a "national home" that would be located within the British protectorate of Palestine. Thereafter, Jewish immigration dramatically affected the demographic composition of that province. As a result, Palestinians found themselves fighting against both the British mandate and the establishment under its aegis of a Jewish homeland on their ancestral territory.

During this last phase of the first Arab Awakening, which lasted for most of the first half of the twentieth century, the various independence struggles took on a distinctly nationalist flavor. Almost all their leaders adopted values that in English would be known as secular. (In Arabic the word is often mistakenly translated to mean "atheist.") Especially after World War I, the dominant European nation-state principle took hold in the region.

Thus, the broader intellectual exploration of the early part of the first Arab Awakening gave way as the movement popularized to a narrower focus on the sole objective of national liberation. As Albert Hourani points out, there were "few precise ideas about social reform and economic development. ... Most of the leaders and spokesmen of the nationalist movements either belonged to families of standing and wealth, or had raised themselves into that class by their own efforts,"[3] and so were less preoccupied by social justice or sustainable economic development. This dearth of attention to the more material challenges facing emerging Arab countries was to prove disastrous for their future evolution—and created the conditions that led to the acute crisis at the end of the first decade of the twenty-first century.

Arab Nationalism After Independence: Dashed Aspirations

The 1940s and 1950s witnessed the emancipation of most Arab countries from colonial rule. The old order was replaced by a variety of postindependence regimes of differing political orientations and outlooks. After replacing republican or monarchist systems, separate factions of the Ba'ath party eventually came to rule Syria and Iraq for the better part of the second half of the twentieth century. The Gulf countries, as well as Jordan and Morocco, opted for the monarchies that still exist today. And Egypt experimented with monarchy before ushering in a republican regime.

Concurrent with the independence movements, however, the other branch of thought—that which emphasized a supranational, pan-Arab identity—was also taking hold. Parties such as the Ba'ath, which originated in Syria in the 1940s and soon spread across the region, promoted the idea of a single Arab nation, despite its fracture into separate local branches.

Tied to this pan-Arab concept, the secularism that it had always implied continued to draw considerable support among the educated Arab elite.

This movement—which coexisted uneasily with the particularist nationalism of the various countries—reached its zenith when a young army officer, Gamal Abdel Nasser, took power in Egypt in the wake of a 1952 military coup that overthrew the monarchy that had replaced British rule in Egypt. Admired as independent of the West, as forcefully standing up to the new Jewish state of Israel, and as embodying the aspirations of the average Arab citizen for dignity, Nasser was claimed as the leader not just of Egypt, but of the whole Arab world. His charisma excited popular adulation across the region. Algerians, for example, though fiercely proud of their particular Algerian identity, adoringly mobbed him when he visited their country shortly after its independence from France in 1962.

Apart from their shared Arab identity, another principle united the citizens of these diverse, newly independent nations: their implacable opposition to the establishment of the state of Israel in their midst in 1948, and their empathy with Palestinians, who, alone among Arab peoples, had had their dreams of independence shattered and had suffered appalling miseries during their expulsion from the land that became Israel. Nasser's famous slogan, "No voice can ring louder than the battle [for the liberation of Palestine]," crystallized this objective as the predominant one for Arab peoples—effectively subordinating all other concerns, including local political reform, until Palestine was liberated.

Herein lay the fatal flaw of the postindependence Arab governments. All the regimes, whether monarchist or "republican," rich or poor, shared one characteristic: none of them paid much attention to developing pluralistic systems of government, building systems of checks and balances on executive power, or promoting the rich diversity of their populations. Instead, the legitimacy gained during independence struggles hardened into diverse forms of autocratic rule. And it was the cry of freedom for Palestinians that allowed these regimes to postpone political reform, as Arab regimes, both friends and foes of Nasser, enthusiastically adopted his slogan in practice if not in name.

The 1967 war with Israel sounded the death knell of the still young pan-Arab nationalist ideal. With the defeat of three Arab states by lone Israel, Nasser's slogans suddenly sounded less like a stirring call for patriotism and more like hollow blandishments that merely served to postpone indefinitely domestic economic development and political reform. With the Arabs' 1967 defeat, it became clear that the Arab world had succeeded with such difficulty in ousting colonial autocracies only to replace them with homegrown ones.

The Rise of Political Islam

The rise of political Islam is often dated slightly later than this period, and is identified with the success of the Iranian revolution in 1979 and with the establishment of the first—and so far the only—theological state in the region (Iran, of course, is not an Arab country). In fact, it was this same 1967 defeat of the Arab countries at the hands of Israel that marked the blossoming of political Islam as a broad-based, competing ideology to pan-Arabism.

The failure to build independent states marked by growing economic prosperity and inclusive political arrangements, coupled with the crushing defeat suffered by the combined

forces of Egypt, Syria, and Jordan after only six days of fighting
—a defeat that, incidentally, led to the occupation of what remained of independent Palestine—struck a crushing blow to
the Arab soul. Arab states tried to downplay the events by referring to the defeat as a mere setback, or *naqsa*.

But it was no use. It had become clear overnight that
rhetoric cannot prevail over preparation when put to the test
in the real world. The euphoria that Nasser and the Syrian
Ba'athist regime could generate with stirring exhortations to
Arab populations burning to liberate Palestine was shattered
by the shocking revelation that beloved Arab leaders had
failed to build modern states that could rise to the occasion. In
this context, political Islam—which was born in Egypt in the
1920s—found a new resonance among a frustrated citizenry.
The values that constituted pan-Arabism began to give way to
a different set of universalist values, based this time in religion.
Political Islam promised cleaner and less self-serving governance on behalf of a population purified by a more rigorous
religious practice. The ascent of political Islam among those
desperate for an alternate paradigm has not slowed to this day.

It did not have to be so. Arab leaders could have acknowledged and absorbed the hard lessons from 1967 and
forged a new work ethic and a framework of accountability
that could serve as the bases for political and social development. They could have built a system of checks and balances
to ensure a democratic, pluralistic system of governance that
could support a fully modern state. But instead, Arab governments clung to authoritarian rule.

In political Islam, moreover, they found a new conve-
nient excuse for keeping their political systems closed. Au-
thoritarians brandished political Islam, both domestically and
to the West, as the bogeyman beside which they cast them-

selves as the lesser of two evils. The West chose conviviality over confrontation with the Arab regimes in exchange for a steady flow of oil and tacit or explicit guarantees of security for Israel. A singular obsession with stability, rather than reform, clouded the lens of Western governments. Most Arab states achieved neither.

In their quest to keep Islamists weak and excluded from the political system, Arab governments and the West inadvertently collaborated to increase their strength. By maintaining exclusive, autocratic political systems, a choice to which the West acquiesced, Arab leaders alienated large segments of the public. Massive inequalities in most Arab societies, created partly by poorly conceived policies but mostly because close-knit elites set about establishing personal control over vast public resources, meant that in the post–1967 war period, impoverished populations found themselves starved simultaneously for bread and freedom. They found no one through whom to express their protest except the Islamists. At the very least, the Islamists promised a more sober lifestyle, greater attention to social justice, and an alternative to the law of unchecked despotism.

Instead of opening the political systems and allowing credible alternatives to emerge, Arab rulers allowed only the Islamists to survive on the margins of the system, thus presenting their citizens with two—often uncomfortable— political choices. Most political Islamist parties in the Arab world were at best ambivalent in their commitment to pluralism. Regimes repeatedly used this authoritarian bent against them—particularly after the Iranian revolution produced a signally repressive regime. It did not matter that pluralism was glaringly absent from the very regimes that were criticizing its lack in Islamist thought. Arab rulers kept waving the red flag of political Islam to inspire fear in their citizens and their Western partners, while their own behavior eroded the credibility of the secularist values upon which their regimes had originally been based.

The Role of the Resource Curse

The Arab world was blessed with one asset that should have bought time for the development of substantive reforms, but it did not. The region's large oil reserves, and the Arab countries' influence over the price of oil since the 1970s, have proved as much a curse as a blessing. Along with the obvious improvements the bonanza brought to the material quality of life in the region, it also gave birth to the "rentier state."

In oil-rich countries, the government made use of its oil income to act as a general provider for its people. Rather than encourage a culture of self-reliance or private sector–led growth, oil state governments fostered a culture of dependency. Citizens came to depend on their rulers to deliver jobs, services, and favors without supplying in return the productivity necessary to develop the economy. Even worse, as governments did not need to raise taxes from their citizens for income, their authoritarianism was more difficult to challenge. The political culture they developed was one of "no taxation, no representation."

It is no coincidence that for many years the most oil-rich countries, such as Saudi Arabia, Qatar, the United Arab Emirates, and Oman, had no elected parliaments. Only recently have these countries introduced limited elections. Even then, as the case of Bahrain has recently revealed, electoral laws often severely distort the representativity of these bodies, and elected members rarely exercise real power or oversight.

The governments of many non-oil-producing countries, such as Jordan, Lebanon, Syria, and Egypt, have come to replicate this system at one step removed. Heavily dependent on aid from oil-producing countries and the West, or on remittances from nationals working in the Gulf, regimes in these non-oil-producing nations could get away with providing fewer social services to their populations while developing their own "semi-rentier" systems. Networks of political elites were cemented around privileges delivered in exchange for loyalty to the regime. Over time, the level of luxury enjoyed by these elite networks, the manifest injustice of resource distribution, resulted in the increasing alienation of the general public.

In a region where 70 percent of the population is under thirty years old, most of today's Arab citizens came of age in an environment acutely lacking in rule of law. The average citizen became almost rest assured that *wasta*—an intermediary with the political elite—was practically the only way to obtain a job or even access to mundane government services. Governments dependent on outside assistance rather than on internally self-sustaining economies nevertheless lived beyond their means. The biggest losers in their societies were productivity, creativity, and a strong work ethic—in other words, the future of their children.

Effect of the Arab-Israeli Conflict

The Arab-Israeli conflict has also served as both an impediment to reform and an excuse for avoiding it. Valuable resources that could otherwise have been channeled into development were spent on security and armaments in the ever tense environment. Moreover, there is no question that authoritarian regimes used the Israeli occupation, illegal as it is, as an excuse for keeping a lid on dissenting citizens who called for reform, and imposing stringent security measures.

For its part, Israel proclaims itself the only democracy in the Middle East and insists it has no partners for peace. However, most of the initiatives over the past decade have come from the Arab side, including the Arab Peace Initiative in 2002 and the Middle East Road Map in 2003. Israel has never put forward its own plan to end the conflict.

As this bruising stalemate has dragged on, the Arab public has lost faith in a peace process that started in Madrid twenty years ago and should have ended in May 1999 with the realization of a two-state solution. Meanwhile, the number of settlers in the West Bank and East Jerusalem has increased from about 250,000, when the Oslo Accords were signed in 1993, to over 500,000 today. While the two sides were still involved in on-again, off-again negotiations, Israel continued to build more settlements and chip away in real terms at the already small territory of land that constitutes the West Bank. By 2012, the Palestinian public in particular and Arabs in general had lost faith in what seems like a perpetual process that only buys Israel time to change conditions on the ground, and actually diminishes the prospects of a Palestinian state free from occupation.

Thus, since the dawn of the first Arab Awakening in the mid-nineteenth century until today, Arab populations have seen the bulk of their aspirations unfulfilled. Though they managed to gain independence from Ottoman and then Western rule, their various hopes—for a modernizing, inclusive polity; administrative and economic reform; and the liberation of the last pocket of Arab population still living under what amounts to colonial occupation—have all come to naught. The level of frustration of Arab populations would be hard to quantify.

The Second Arab Awakening

In December 2010 a street vendor named Muhammad Bouazizi set himself on fire in the underprivileged inland Tunisian
town of Sidi Bouzid. What pushed him over the edge seems to
have been one of the all-too-frequent attempts by the police to
shake him down in return for permission to park his cart. But
really, of course, Bouazizi was protesting the degrading conditions of his entire life.

That life seemed to incarnate the cumulative failures of
the first Arab Awakening. He had no prospects for a job that
could provide him economic security, living day to day on
the proceeds of miserable street sales; he had no say in political affairs, and he suffered daily humiliating abuse at the
hands of agents of the very government that was supposed
to provide for him. Surely this is not the result dreamed by
either George Antonius or Ibrahim Yazegi when he exhorted
Arabs to arise and awake. Surely this is not the result that Tunisia's Constitution Party or neighboring Algerian freedom
fighters had struggled for. Bouazizi ignited more than an uprising. He lit a spark to decades' worth of the dry tinder of
frustration and humiliation that had been stockpiling across
the region. The movement he catalyzed swept across an Arab
world that had remained dormant through decades of authoritarian rule and state abuses.

One can endlessly debate why this particular incident
triggered a massive conflagration across a region that had for
so long been resistant to political change. Regardless of the
reason, the notoriously fragmented Arab world was suddenly
unified, with protests in monarchies and republics alike, in
wealthy and poor countries—everywhere that Arab governments had ruled a seemingly acquiescent and docile public. It

no longer matters whether these governments were truly blind to the simmering resentment or had simply chosen to ignore it, believing they could keep it under control. Once the streets erupted in protest, it quickly became apparent that most Arab governments' decades-old reflex of delaying and deflecting political reform would no longer be an option.

Few nations can claim to have predicted this chain of events—or to have adopted successful policies in response. Neither Arab governments nor the United States, Europe, or Israel can claim to have made a contribution to tackling the main issues confronting the region: stability, democracy, peace, and economic opportunity. All these countries have contributed to stagnation and societal breakdown. All need new thinking, and new policies.

In the three years that have passed since this second Arab Awakening began, it has now become obvious that the process it set in motion has only begun. The latest Arab uprisings brought to the fore long-standing issues of reform, stability, and peace—objectives still sought by Arabs and the West alike. Yet what the uprisings have shown is that the tactics used to meet these objectives must change. Several myths have been shattered already: that food must be put on the table before political reform can move forward; that peaceful change in this region is not possible; that the notion of "moderation" can be selectively applied to regimes' attitude to Israel, but not to their politics; and that any change will inevitably bring radical political Islam to power.

The Real Change

Now the hard part begins. The region is just beginning to confront its challenges. The Arab world needs to develop truly pluralistic systems in which all political forces, including Islamist ones, can operate, but none can monopolize power. It must establish economic models that work for the general public, not just an elite few. It must create education systems that teach people to be true citizens rather than subjects. And it must find peace within each Arab society, as well as between Arabs and Israelis. Until these challenges are met, the promise that the transitions in the Middle East hold will be just as disappointed as was the promise of the first Arab Awakening.

As a partner in this process, the West must disabuse itself of the idea that stability can be achieved by prioritizing it as an objective over that of political reform. Most important, however, both Arab states and the West must understand that they no longer have the luxury of time to solve the region's long-standing problems. That luxury disappeared once the street decided to set its own pace.

Traditional thinking about the Arab-Israeli conflict must also give way to the realities of a new Middle East. In the United States, the peace process has largely been seen through the prism of Israel. American support for freedom for Jews seemed to ignore or bypass the Palestinians' legitimate desire for their own freedom—and, by extension, the Arabs' desire for a resolution of the conflict. This outdated reasoning must be revised, and the Israeli occupation needs to end. The Palestinian street will probably not wait for the United States or Israel to decide when the time is right to solve the conflict, at a time when change is being effected by several Arab publics around it.

Fear is not the only barrier that has been broken by these uprisings. A sense of powerlessness permeated the Arab world for decades, leaving ordinary citizens feeling they had no choice but to submit to policies made by either their governments or the outside world. Those feelings are gone. With time for a two-state solution quickly running out, a speedy and just settlement is in everyone's interest. The United States, in particular, would be ill-advised to wait for more favorable conditions to emerge at some later date. If there is no movement toward peace as new Arab democracies take shape, negative views of Israel and the West will harden at a time when Arab public opinion is gaining influence. Given that the new governments are less forgiving than old ones about Israel's occupation of Palestinian lands, the United States could watch its influence in the new Middle East sharply wane.

Israel also needs to revisit its policies. As Arab political reform progresses, Israel's claim to be the only democracy in the Middle East will ring increasingly false. With conditions changing on the ground, it will be harder to ignore Palestinians' pressing demands for independence. If new democracies see the Israeli government impeding a viable and dignified resolution of the Arab-Israeli conflict, Israel's concern that the region will grow more hostile will become a self-fulfilling prophecy. On the other hand, a process undertaken in partnership with elected and thus legitimate Arab governments will reinforce long-term peace and stability. Those who argue that peacemaking cannot be successful in a time of flux ignore the fact that it is precisely in these times that dramatic breakthroughs can occur—and that outsiders can help shape the process.

Real Change Takes Time

The tumultuous events of 2011 and their aftermath can clearly be deemed a second Arab Awakening. Unlike the first, it began as a popular, not an elite, movement. It still needs to be contextualized within a coherent intellectual framework. The challenge, in other words, is to make sure it does not end as the first one did—in shattered dreams and the replacement of one set of autocratic rulers with another. If any lesson is to be learned from recent Arab history, it is that the downfall of autocratic leaders and systems is not enough to achieve freedom and prosperity. Great care and attention must be given to what replaces them. Rather than grasping for power, successor forces must display the restraint, foresight, imagination, and effort required to build resilient, accountable, and democratic systems of governance.

This profound sociopolitical process needed the dramatic flare of Bouazizi's match to commence, but it will unfold over decades rather than over months or years. This timeline should come as no surprise. From the outbreak of hostilities in 1775 to the ratification of the Constitution in 1789, the American Revolution achieved a functioning, independent, and democratic political order only after a course of some fifteen years—and this occurred in a remarkably homogeneous political and cultural environment. Europe's emancipation from authoritarian rule evolved over several centuries. It is sometimes easy to forget that Germany was a totalitarian state as recently as 1945; and Poland broke free only in 1989. Spain, Portugal, and Greece shook off authoritarian rule only in the 1970s and 1980s. Chile and Argentina were still dictatorships until almost 1990. Japan received its first democratic constitution in the late 1940s. The list goes on. In the dizzyingly heterogeneous Arab world, ruling establishments have always ensured that political parties and civil society organizations were suppressed. As a result, few alternative leaders or systems have evolved the capacity to take over from fallen autocrats.

The only logical course for Arab governments to take

is to not stand in the way but to try to ensure that the second Arab Awakening does not fizzle. No matter which political systems Arab countries adopt, the Arab world will miss a golden opportunity if it does not give diversity and pluralism the attention they deserve. This applies to civil and religious forces alike. A new culture needs to be nurtured. No individual or party can claim monopoly on the truth and still expect a prosperous society to emerge.

In short, the only way for Arab governments—new and old—to maintain power will be to share it. Absolute power has ceased to be an option. For both civil and religious parties, the commitment to pluralism must be unambiguous, permanent, and irreversible.

2

Redefining Arab Moderation

In the decades following independence, most of the Arab world lived in a state of artificially induced stability. The opposition, mostly Islamist since the 1970s, was kept outside the system. Meanwhile, Arab regimes ruled by force, giving the international community, and part of their populations, the false sense that their societies were stable and had ample time to develop economically before contemplating serious political transformations. The West was prepared to ignore the issue of political reform. It coined the phrase "Arab moderates" to describe Arab regimes in Egypt, Jordan, Saudi Arabia, and elsewhere that did not advance political reform but that did pursue or support peace with Israel. Countries that did not pursue a peaceful solution to the Arab-Israeli conflict—that either advocated, supported, or engaged in violence to end the Israeli occupation—were labeled hard-liners. This included Syria and nonstate actors like Hamas and Hezbollah.

But the word "moderate" does not necessarily apply to those regimes if one looks beyond the Arab-Israeli peace process and examines the broader challenges facing the Arab world today. The Arab Awakening has highlighted this dichotomy. Saudi Arabia's record on political and cultural diversity, representative government, and women's rights, for example, does not suggest a moderate, reformist approach. The fall of Hosni Mubarak in Egypt has brought to light the practices of a regime that stifled political life for decades, often brutally. Suddenly, the world came to abhor the practices of a regime it had considered moderate simply because of its position on peace with Israel. Ordinary Egyptians did not look at their regime as moderate, and the world cheered with them as they poured into Tahrir Square and demanded their freedom and dignity.

While the "moderates" of the Arab world were trying and failing to resolve the Arab-Israeli conflict, they ignored the other critical challenges of state building. They did not achieve either peace abroad or reform at home. Until 2011, it was difficult to point to any Arab country and label its governance truly moderate.

Syria, for example, neither preaches nor practices moderation. But the Syrian regime's "hard-line" position on the peace process pales in comparison to its position on reform, which has brought death to thousands of its own people. The Syrian regime was able to sell its hard-line position on the peace process to segments of its own society, and to the Arab world generally, as an indication that it understood and respected its people's aspirations. Of course, wide sectors of Syrian society recognized this deception and took to the streets after decades of oppression.

The regime's claim to be in tune with its people's aspirations clashed with the slaughter of its own citizens, and support for the Syrian regime has plummeted, not just inside Syria but throughout the Arab world. In a 2009 survey of more than four thousand Arabs in Morocco, Egypt, Lebanon,

Jordan, Saudi Arabia, and the United Arab Emirates, Bashar Assad scored higher than any other Arab head of state as a respected leader from another country and was the secondmost respected leader internationally, tied with Jacques Chirac.[1] In contrast, when polling was done again in 2011, the vast majority of people in the same six countries did not believe Assad could still govern Syria. In Morocco, the country that viewed him most favorably, 85 percent of respondents considered his rule illegitimate.[2]

One clear implication of the changes sweeping the Arab world today is that the notion of Arab "moderation" needs to be redefined to include domestic issues such as political diversity, religious tolerance, and inclusiveness. The principal yardstick should therefore measure whether regimes enjoy legitimacy with their publics, whether they are building representative systems that are more responsive to their people, whether power is shared among all branches of government rather than monopolized by the executive, and whether the rights of all citizens, including those of ethnic and religious minorities as well as women, are guaranteed.

Such a definition will surely complicate many Arab countries' relationships with the West, which has tended to wink at authoritarian practices as long as the regimes pursued Arab-Israeli peace. The West will consequently be forced to reach some accommodation with political Islam in the Arab world. But such a situation will translate into a more stable and enduring relationship.

It will also serve the cause of peace—not a forced peace but an agreement that would end the Israeli occupation and guarantee the right of Palestinians to their own state. Under such a scenario, where Lebanon and Palestine have the legitimacy and mandate to exercise sovereignty over their own territories, armed organizations like Hamas and Hezbollah would no longer have reason to exist. They would have to evolve into purely political forces that exercise their right to effect policy peacefully, much as the Irish Republican Army (IRA) and other armed groups evolved after the peace agreement was reached in Ireland.

Before the Arab Awakening, the only real options for governance in the Arab world were the traditional political elites or forces that used religion for partisan purposes. Both made many Arabs uncomfortable because they lacked an unequivocal (or frequently any) commitment to democracy. Several works have shown that Arabs regard democracy as the best form of government—and that they understand what it means.[3] The Arab uprisings gave many people hope that the bipolar monopoly of the ruling elite and the Islamists finally would be broken, and that the democracy gap could be filled by third forces.

The Elite's Resistance to Reform

Arab governments—unfettered by a free press, opposition parties, or a vibrant civil society—have grown increasingly closed over the years. The four Arab leaders who were forced out of power since the start of the Arab uprisings (Ben Ali in Tunisia, Mubarak in Egypt, Qadhafi in Libya, and Saleh in Yemen) spent a total of one hundred and thirty years in power, an average of a little more than thirty-two years each. During their tenures, opposition parties were either banned or heavily suppressed.

In Arab governments the increasingly insular political elite have often hardened into a tightly linked cronyism, monopolizing wide sectors of the economy. Along with this political-economic constriction have come increased public perception of high levels of corruption. In the Transparency International "Corruption Perceptions Index" of 2011, of the one hundred and eighty-two countries ranked worldwide, thirteen Arab countries were ranked eightieth or higher (the smaller the number the lower the level of perceived corruption), including Egypt, Syria, Yemen, and Libya. Tunisia was ranked seventy-third.[4]

Resistance to meaningful reform is not limited to Arab rulers. Much of it comes from the political and business elite. This class is eager to protect its privileges and the opportunity to extract resources under a rentier system whose ruling cliques buy loyalty, or at least quiescence, with such favors. This group has become so entrenched and so ossified that it has no qualms about turning against its own benefactors when its interests are threatened, as, for example, when some Arab leaders contemplate even limited reform measures.[5]

These political and business elites are present in several Arab countries that are currently experiencing transitions, including Egypt, Tunisia, and Syria. Like the rulers whose favors it has enjoyed, this elite class has also used the ascendance of political Islam as a scare tactic, both domestically and internationally. Its argument is simple and effective: if you open up the system, the Islamists will take over.

Even when elections take place—such as the November 2010 parliamentary polls in Egypt, and in Jordan at the eve of the Arab uprisings—the framework in which they are held is designed to protect the elite by producing weak and subservient parliaments rather than bodies that exercise true oversight of the executive branch of government. Parliaments in the Arab world were never intended to share power with the executive branch or hold it in check. Instead, they created a façade of democracy intended to impress citizens and the outside world while insulating the regimes from pressure for genuine reform. But 2011 ended this charade. No one is fooled anymore by the idea that elections are synonymous with reform or democracy. Many have attributed the start of the revolution in Egypt to the November 2010 elections, which produced a parliament with no opposition members. The Egyptian public could not stomach being taken for fools yet again.

Another complicating factor is brain drain. Many of the most educated members of Arab society—a group that likely would be involved in effecting change—have emigrated in search of opportunities elsewhere. According to the 2010–2011 Global Competitiveness Report of the World Economic Forum, the Arab countries that have experienced the highest levels of brain drain are Libya, Algeria, Syria, and Egypt, ranking 134th, 125th, 118th, and 114th, respectively, out of a total 139 countries (the higher the number, the greater the brain-drain).[6] Among these countries, Algeria is the only one that experienced a major conflict in the past forty years, so the common factor appears not to be war—the usual suspect—but the inefficiency of the state system and the humiliations and frustrations it imposes on its people. According to the National Arab American Medical Association, close to fifteen thousand physicians who graduated from Arab medical schools now reside and practice in the United States.[7] Partly as a consequence of this brain drain, the Arab world has fallen behind almost every other region in terms of overall human development, socioeconomic stability, and political reform.

The Rise of Religious Parties

As the elite's privileges expanded, so too did its interest in protecting them. Self-aggrandizement superseded loyalty to the state or to merit as a virtue. With economic liberalization (which occurred to varying degrees in different countries) and the growing coziness of business-regime relations, the state began losing one of its major legitimizing tools: its postindependence commitment to social programs, including education and health services.

Religious parties thus found two voids to fill: one was the abandonment of the social terrain by ruling cliques increasingly interested in lining their own pockets, and the other was the political void created by the suppression of secular opposition. These groups benefited from the fact that most Arab states were social-authoritarian in their structure, meaning that at some point in the past they derived their legitimacy from social and welfare programs. As that function declined, Islamist parties managed to siphon off some of the governments' legitimacy by complementing or taking over the state's role in providing public services.

Through their philanthropy and social services, religious-based parties obtained a granular understanding of their populations and constructed a broad and deep base of support. By the time some Arab regimes contemplated limited political reforms, religious groups had already established a significant edge over other civil society organizations in connecting with ordinary people. The latter had difficulty gaining traction for a variety of reasons, including continued repression by the regime. The Tunisian government under Ben Ali, for example, systematically prevented the development of any freely constituted network of associations or interest groups mediating between society and the political system. Independent representation of interests was consistently obstructed by hurdles such as the required approval by the ministry of interior and restrictions on the freedom of speech and the media.[8]

The political immobility that was originally intended to

preserve the status quo for the elites and later to shield society against radical ideologies instead had the opposite effect. Many Arab publics increasingly regarded the ruling elite as aloof and unaccountable rather than as "moderate," and viewed religious groups as more sympathetic and responsive. Secular groups, meanwhile, were often either elitist, disengaged from effective constituent politics, or suppressed by governments and thus seen by the public as marginal. This experience suggests a counterargument bolstering calls for pluralistic reform in the Arab world: if the system is *not* opened up, only the Islamists can garner mass support.

The Need for Third Forces

There is no excuse for this state of affairs. Where other regions have learned to face their challenges and move ahead—even if those challenges are not as formidable as the Arab-Israeli conflict—the Arab world maintained that its special circumstances should excuse it from meaningful reform. As the UN Arab Human Development Report of 2002 demonstrates, Arab countries had the lowest "freedom score" in the late 1990s out of seven world regions, and the lowest average value of voice and accountability of all world regions.[9] Tunisia's revolt seemed to signal to Arab governments that public patience was at an end and that time—previously considered an infinite commodity that afforded Arab regimes endless opportunities to stall serious reform—had abruptly run out.

Arab regimes' verbal commitments to processes that will lead to democracy have rarely been accompanied by practical steps. The political economies over which they preside have been increasingly contaminated by corruption, and their record on efficient delivery of services leaves much to be desired.

The Islamist opposition, on the other hand, has not demonstrated a clear commitment to pluralism, peaceful alternation of power, or individual rights, and its governing record in
Egypt and Tunisia so far seems to back secular forces' claims
that such a commitment to pluralism is shaky at best. It is still
not categorically clear whether these parties see democracy as
a principle or as a temporary and expendable tool to be used
to gain power that they then deny to others. Their promises to
effectively address Arab societies' problems need to be put to
the test. Although they have efficiently delivered some social
welfare, their proposed solutions to economic challenges seldom go beyond generalities. The slogan "Islam is the solution"
remains to be translated into specific, implementable policies
for challenges such as unemployment, lagging productivity,
and budget deficits.

The Arab Awakening has clearly demonstrated that the
commitment to democratic norms by both the Islamists and
the secular elements—the old regimes as well as those emerging as third forces—is still only skin-deep. Many of the secular forces still appear more "liberal" (open-minded about
social and economic issues) than democratic (committed
to the right of all political forces, including the Islamists, to
be included in the political process). Their fear of the Islamists clearly trumps their belief in democratic principles. The
Islamists, while clearly having adjusted their positions to assure society that they are democratic, have yet to match their
verbal commitments with actions on the ground. Commitments to individual and women's rights, for example, by the
Muslim Brotherhood—and particularly by the Salafis—are far
less than categorical. We have yet to see whether these forces
will become more or less democratic with time. However,

many still see this battle as a zero-sum game rather than as a fight for pluralism from which all can benefit.

There is a dire need in the Arab world for political forces that are as passionate about reform as they are about peaceful methods, as insistent about political and cultural diversity as they are about advancing their own positions. Such a discourse has been largely absent from Arab politics for decades, but not from the minds and hearts of Arab citizens. But we cannot expect it to develop overnight after authoritarian regimes have artificially closed the political and cultural space in the Arab world for so long. A pluralistic movement truly committed to all the principles of democracy—majority rule and minority rights, individual freedoms, human rights, a robust free press, peaceful alternation of power through free and fair elections, rule of law, and equality for men and women—cannot emerge in the absence of a political culture that encourages diversity; an educational system that teaches it; a civil society that lobbies and monitors the executive; or the institutional capacity for all of the above.

The only way to allow for such a third way to develop is to open the political space. The short-term implication is that the Islamists will benefit from the credibility they earned through their oppression at the hands of the old regimes, decades of being demonized by the West, and the lack of a requirement to develop political platforms beyond slogans like "Islam is the solution." Various polls show that for decades popular support for the Islamists in Egypt, Tunisia, Morocco, and Jordan hovered around 15 to 20 percent. In the absence of other political parties with similar organizational capabilities, they have been able to translate this support into much higher representation in emerging systems. But even if Islamist parties gain an initial advantage, they are unlikely to keep it if they fail to respond to their peoples' aspirations.

Today a unique window of opportunity has opened to spur a new discourse that depicts diversity as a source of strength, not weakness: an irreplaceable asset to the region's economic, social, and intellectual development. But it will take time for such a discourse, and the cultural underpinnings that nourish it, to develop.

The romantic notion that emerged just after the Tunisian uprising—that such a transformation would be automatic and immediate—is what created the misnomer "the Arab Spring." This concept has given way to reality; while the change in the Arab world is deep and permanent, we are witnessing only the first chapter in a metamorphosis that will take decades. The frustrations festered for decades and are well defined. People know what the protesters are against: despotic leaders, corruption, daily humiliations, inequitable and inefficient delivery of services, lack of jobs, a poor quality of life, ineffective governance, and lack of attention to merit. But the demonstrators have not been equally clear on what they stand for. They have made general demands for dignity, freedom, and a better life, with little articulation of how to achieve these aims. Such an articulation will take time, education, and much trial and error before it crystallizes.

One phenomenon that may draw the process out is polarization. In many parts of the Arab world the fight has sadly developed into one between the "liberals" or the "secularists" vs. the "Islamists," with the Islamists (for now) coming out decidedly on top. The two camps seem to view the contest as a zero-sum game—one side's win must be the other's loss. It is not just the Islamists who have been antipluralist: the secular forces, in and outside of power, have likewise been vocal in their opposition to Islamist political participation. An International Crisis Group (ICG) Egypt Conflict Alert summarized the situation aptly when it noted the existence of "a persistent, perilous standoff between on one side the president and his Islamist backers for whom elections appear to mean everything, and, on the other, opposition forces for whom they seem to mean nothing."[10]

Both sides have understandable fears. The Islamists have just come through a long desert of repression, in which they did not have access to political space, and in many cases suffered the physical brutality of the old regimes. They feel a strong temptation to protect themselves in the future by guaranteeing their domination of political space. The secularists, on the other hand, look at the exclusionist language of Islamist movements and the experience in such countries as Iran, Afghanistan, and even parts of Algeria and assume the intention hiding beneath the Islamists' conciliatory rhetoric is to consolidate power so as to exclude everyone else. Zeyneb Farhat, director of Tunisia's national theater, bitterly complained that Ennahda, Tunisia's largest Islamist party, which won a plurality in Tunisia's elections, is not a moderate party despite the reporting by most Western journalists. "Let me tell you, no body at the United States Embassy in Tunisia was informed. Nobody. That's why Hillary Clinton twice told Ennahda that their merchandise is not what was sold a few months ago in order to get support from the American administration."[11]

That is the wrong way to view or engage in such a fight. The absence of an institutional culture that will allow a democracy with enough room for Islamists, liberals, and all the other political forces implies that even before the fight for power another battle must be fought: the battle for pluralism. Otherwise, politics will consist of a fight between two ideological camps, each working to exclude the other entirely, often adopting positions that are inherently undemocratic. Both forces need to show the courage to forgo absolute power, because only in that way can both gain the right to exist in perpetuity and save their populations from an endless cycle of tit-for-tat authoritarianism.

A raw struggle for power will not lead to any appreciation of diversity and its benefits or respect for other points of view and the valuable innovations they may contain. One cannot be selectively democratic, opting for it only when it brings the desired electoral results. If the fight is for pluralism, then both the liberals and the Islamists have a shared interest in laying the institutional groundwork that will guarantee all groups the right to organize and operate free of intervention. This is the only principle that preserves both the Islamist and the secular forces' interests.

Are such third forces emerging from the Arab Awakening? Are we witnessing the internalization by Arab publics that something needs to be done to break the monopoly of the two dominant forces in the region? Is it premature to expect this? Will the Arab world take the opportunity to establish pluralism as a new basis for the architecture of sustainable development? Or will this post-2011 moment be yet another false start, full of promise but degenerating into civil strife, autocratic regimes, and monopolies on truth?

If the idea of third forces truly committed to democratic principles has not taken hold yet, it does not mean they might not emerge. The Arab Awakening has given these forces a chance by allowing a long-awaited battle of ideas to begin. This is the battle that will decide whether the region will arrive at a true moderation, committed to pluralistic principles at all times. To presume a priori that this battle will end either badly, with the replacement of one set of despots by another, or brilliantly, with pluralistic cultures, is naive. The truth will probably lie somewhere in between, with different Arab countries developing at different paces, and with different degrees of success—or failure.

3

Islamist Movements

Despots or Democrats

E ven though Iran is not an Arab country, the overthrow of its shah in 1979 catapulted the issue of political Islam onto center stage in the Arab world. The
euphoria the revolution generated in countries suffering under authoritarian regimes quickly gave way to disappoint-
ment as one dictatorship was replaced by another. The revolution
introduced the first—and only—theocracy in the Middle East.

Iran adopted Ruhollah Khomeini's interpretation of the
Shia doctrine "Wilayet Al Faqih" (Guardianship of the Jurist),
which gives the Islamic jurist custodianship over the people.
In the months following the revolution, all secular parties were
banned; tolerance of different religious communities, including Christian and Baha'i, was curtailed; personal rights were
compromised; and a dual system of government was introduced, part religious and part civil, in which the former always
took precedence over the latter. Most people in the region and
beyond saw this system, still in practice today, as a harbinger
of what would take place if Islamist parties were to come to
power elsewhere. The West's fears were enhanced in the 1980s

by the emergence of armed Islamic resistance groups such as Hamas in the Occupied Palestinian Territories and Hezbollah in Lebanon—both directly or indirectly supported by Iran.

These developments made Arab governments, secular groups, and the international community see an emerging threat from an armed, radical, and absolutist political Islam. This new movement seemed prepared to use democracy to gain power, then to stifle diversity and subsequently deny others the right to a peaceful rotation of power through elections. Former U.S. Assistant Secretary of State Edward Djerjian dubbed the strategy "One man, one vote, one time."[1]

The emergence of Al-Qaeda and the horrific attacks of September 11, 2001, seemed to resolve any doubts about the Islamists' objectives. Many came to see political Islam as a doctrine aimed at killing people and obliterating diversity. At least until the second Arab Awakening, Arab governments used this perception of Islamists as a scare tactic to hold on to power and to present themselves, both to their populaces and to the West, as the bulwarks against radical Islam.

With all of their differences, however, the Iranian regime, Al-Qaeda, Hamas, Hezbollah, and even Algeria's radical Islamist party, the FIS, do not accurately represent political Islam. There are other groups, and they tell a different story. Do all Islamist groups regard religion as the final arbiter, a stance that is incompatible with political diversity and democratic norms? When voters turn to Islamists, are they voting for the piousness or perceived cleanliness of the candidates, for the platform of the movement, or to protest the establishment? Is a vote for Islamist movements also a vote against democracy?

The debate on this issue has been highly charged and simplistic. Many adopt black-and-white positions: political Islam either is an evil that must be fought at all times or has all the answers to the problems of a region long ruled by autocratic, unresponsive regimes. A more objective look at political Islam must begin by examining its different groups, ideologies, and commitment—or lack thereof—to democratic principles.

Political Islam Is Not Monolithic

While major differences exist between armed Islamist groups —Al-Qaeda is clearly distinct from Hezbollah and Hamas— these groups generally color most people's views of political Islam. The fact is, however, that these groups represent only a small minority within the overall universe of political Islam. Most of today's political Islam can be traced back to a group called the Muslim Brotherhood, founded in Egypt in 1928 with offshoots later established in many Arab countries. In almost all cases, the Muslim Brotherhood and its offshoots have re-nounced violence and now aspire to achieve their social and political objectives peacefully. Even within the various Muslim Brotherhood organizations, views on political diversity differ from country to country.

To better understand the differences within political Is-lam, groups can be divided into four main movements: vio-lent and exclusionary, militant resistance, Salafis, and peace-ful.[2] I have established these categories for analytical clarity, but human motivations are never perfectly unambiguous and there is a degree of overlap and permeability among some of these groups.

VIOLENT, EXCLUSIONIST MOVEMENTS

The violent Islamist groups refuse to work within established systems. They reject participation in all domestic political processes and adopt a *takfiri* ideology, branding as an infidel any individual or group that does not agree with their views—

regardless of whether they are Muslims, Arabs, or foreigners —and believing that killing these people is legitimate. These groups regard themselves as the true representatives of Islam and claim a monopoly on understanding (and enforcing) Islamic law. They see themselves engaged in a global struggle against any society that does not subscribe to their values. Their theater of battle is the entire world, including Muslim societies that they consider un-Islamic. Al-Qaeda falls into this category.

This group is not only the smallest of all Islamist groups but also the least credible among Muslims. Whereas members of this group thrive on abusive regimes, chaos, and instability —such as in Afghanistan, Iraq, and Yemen—their brutal methods, exclusionist ideologies, and often indiscriminately violent actions have alienated them from the overwhelming majority of the Muslim population. Iraqis, having experienced their violent behavior, rose up against the local Al-Qaeda subsidiary in 2007. The movement was on the wane in Iraq following the death of Abu Musab al-Zarqawi, its local leader.

The beginning of the Arab Awakening in December 2010 signaled a further loss for this brand of political Islam, because the popular revolts challenged the idea that change can be realized only through violence. The killing of Osama Bin Laden was another blow. There are indications that Al-Qaeda and its affiliates have learned from their mistakes and may be adapting to the new environment. Some violent attacks in the Sinai, Libya, and Syria are attributed to Al-Qaeda members, as the movement exploits opportunities in drawn-out conflict and residual chaos. It may also be forging alliances with some of the Salafi parties that have sprung up in Tunisia and Egypt. And it seems to be expanding around the edges of the Muslim world, with newly powerful affiliates in Nigeria and Mali. Still, at the moment, the extreme, violent fringe represented by Al-Qaeda does not hold sway within the heartland.

MILITANT RESISTANCE MOVEMENTS

Resistance groups see violence, including violence against civilians, as a means to national liberation. Their activities are usually confined to national territories under occupation and to the territory of the occupier. Hamas[3] in the West Bank and Gaza, and Hezbollah in Lebanon, are prime examples.

While they established themselves to work outside of the system, these groups are increasingly participants in elections, even as they continue to carry arms. The issue of their weapons has become a point of contention in Palestinian and Lebanese societies, as well as in the international community. Hamas's acts of violence have largely stopped in recent years due to an understanding with Israel and a realization that the majority of Palestinians oppose attacks against civilians. In Lebanon there are worries that Hezbollah will use its arms against fellow Lebanese citizens rather than against Israel.

Although neither group has officially renounced violence, Hamas and Hezbollah have chosen to participate with other political groups in the political systems of their state (or proto-state). A resolution of the Arab-Israeli conflict along the lines of the Arab Peace Initiative will make it difficult for either group to retain its arms, and they may then operate as purely political organizations, even if their commitment to democratic norms might still be suspect.

SALAFIS

Salafis do not follow one leader or belong to one political party. "Salafi" is a catchall term for individuals who adhere to a strict interpretation of Islam and who seek to return to Islam as it was practiced under the Prophet Muhammad and the first generations of his followers. Although Salafi groups have existed for years in some Arab countries, they were not involved in electoral politics until after the Arab Awakenings. Salafi groups include those that believe in violence as well as those that advocate peaceful change.

In the past, authoritarian regimes such as Mubarak's in Egypt encouraged these groups as an alternative to the Muslim Brotherhood because their puritan version of Islam advocates total obedience to the ruler. Today, however, the Salafis' successes in Egypt as well as their increasing visibility in Tunisia have generated fears that they will attempt to impose their religious views on all citizens. It is not yet clear whether they are a permanent movement in the Arab and Islamic worlds.

In June 2012 I met with Imad El Din Abdel Ghaffour, then the chairman of Al-Nour, the largest Salafi party in Egypt, and he flatly denied that his party would force its religious views on citizens. He said his party is committed to political pluralism and a peaceful rotation of power at all times. "He who accepts to be part of the political system has to accept its results," he told me, adding that it is inconceivable that his party would impose a dress code or a certain way of life on Egyptians. Al-Nour, he said, accepted the Azhar document, a text negotiated and agreed to by a wide spectrum of civil leaders and religious scholars in June 2011. This agreement called for a civil state, guaranteed protections for minority and individual rights, a commitment to pluralism, and a peaceful alternation of power. It remains to be seen whether these positions will be implemented, given the group's earlier position calling for the establishment of an Islamic caliphate. Salafi groups in Tunisia have clearly resorted to violence, and there is potential for mutual support between some Salafis and Al-Qaeda leadership and offshoots.

PEACEFUL MOVEMENTS

The largest category of Islamists consists of groups that have decided to seek power through participation in elections and spread their ideologies peacefully. Most of these groups are offshoots of the Muslim Brotherhood. They all share one trait: they have made clear their belief in a peaceful process of political change. Their commitment to political pluralism and personal rights is more nuanced, however, depending on each group's particular evolution in its own country.

I will focus on four such movements in detail: the Muslim Brotherhood in Egypt and Jordan; its offshoots in Tunisia and Morocco; Ennahda; and the Party for Justice and Development. Because of their electoral success, observers are closely scrutinizing their positions on three issues: political pluralism, including their acceptance of the principle of a peaceful rotation of power; minority and individual rights and freedoms; and economic programs.

The Freedom and Justice Party

Egypt's Muslim Brotherhood is the mother of all Muslim Brotherhood movements. Established in 1928 by Hasan Al-Banna, a schoolteacher and religious leader, to promote personal piety and charitable activities, it put forth candidates in Egypt's 1941 elections. As it evolved, it was implicated in some acts of violence, particularly between the 1940s and the 1960s. Officials attributed a failed assassination attempt on Egyptian president Gamal Abdel Nasser in October 1954 to the Muslim Brotherhood, leading the Egyptian authorities to imprison many of the Brotherhood's members and outlaw the group. While the Muslim Brotherhood in Egypt now acknowledges its past violence against the state, the group abandoned these tactics in the 1970s and dismisses them today as unauthorized.[4] The Muslim Brotherhood has been criticized by more radical Islamists around the world for its denunciation of violence.

As the oldest Islamist movement in the contemporary Arab world, the Brotherhood in Egypt has seen many leaders and has experienced a wide range of ruling regimes. Accordingly, its position on political participation, pluralism, and personal rights has gone through a few iterations. It assumed its most hard-line stances on these issues when Sayyed Qutub was one of its leading members in the 1950s and 1960s. While Qutub has become an iconic figure among radical Islamists, the mainstream of the Muslim Brotherhood has decisively rejected those ideas. Its commitment to pluralism and personal rights is still seen by many as less categorical and even undemocratic. Yet there is no doubt that its positions on these issues have become more moderate, particularly since the 1980s, when members of the Brotherhood, running as independents, were elected to the Egyptian parliament. Since then they have had to operate as a political party, cooperating with other political actors to reach compromises, rather than as a religious organization with unbending ideological views.

One study explains that "the central objective of the contemporary Brotherhood continues to be the establishment of an Islamic state that is governed not by human, man-made laws, but by the *sharia*."[5] It adds that Brotherhood leaders do not insist on a state governed by them personally, as long as it is governed by someone who will uphold Islamic concepts. The Brotherhood in Egypt and elsewhere has always insisted that such an Islamic state can be arrived at only through persuasion, not coercion, of the populace, according to the Qur'anic verse "La ikraha fil deen" (no compulsion in religion).[6]

That broad objective, however, leaves many questions

unanswered. What are the contours of sharia law, and what would it look like? Will it be the only source of legislation, with all laws derived from it? Do sharia laws need to be imposed on all citizens, with no room for personal choice? Do the apostasy laws apply to politics? According to many contemporary interpretations, there is no compulsion for people to enter into Islam, but once they do they are not allowed to leave the religion without being considered infidels who are subject to punishment (scholars disagree on the type of punishment).[7] This principle has political implications. If citizens are persuaded to choose an Islamic state, are they allowed to change their mind subsequently and vote the Islamists out? Or does the Brotherhood believe the road to the Islamic state is one-directional? Since the Brotherhood has formed political parties in many Arab countries, everyone is watching to see if its participation in electoral politics will mean compromising its ideological positions and accepting the democratic principle that the ballot box alone decides who comes in and who goes out of power.

The Grand Imam of Al-Azhar, Ahmad Al-Tayyeb, told me that Muslim scholars differ over the theological rule of "no compulsion in religion," and that the Qur'an itself does not have any text on punishing those who opt out of Islam. He also pointed out that only two hadiths (sayings by Prophet Muhammad) refer to "apostasy." Scholars' opinions range widely. Some argue that people who opt out of Islam must be killed; others, like Sheikh Rached Al-Ghannouchi, the leader of Ennahda in Tunisia, argue that it is not for "man" but rather for God to pass judgment on their actions.

The Brotherhood in Egypt attempted to articulate its position in 2007, in a draft party platform that, because of internal differences, was never published. While the draft showed respect for political liberties, including those of women, it was less than totally committed to democratic principles on social and cultural issues.[8] For instance, it stated that women and non-Muslims must be excluded from senior government positions. Recently, however, as the Muslim Brotherhood has become the major political party in Egypt, it has dropped this restriction from its program.

After Mubarak was unseated in February 2011, the Muslim Brotherhood decided to form a political party and enter the elections. The Brotherhood's Freedom and Justice Party (FJP) proceeded to win 43.4 percent of the vote, or 216 seats out of the 498 in the People's Assembly.[9] The party ran on a published platform that addressed a wide range of issues, including political participation, personal and minority rights, and economic policies.

This platform was a significant departure from earlier Brotherhood positions. It articulated the group's adherence to democratic principles of government, although not enough to classify the movement as a wholly democratic one.[10] While it affirmed its allegiance to the principle of a civil state and defined such a state as one that is not run by the military or the religious clergy, it reiterated the view that Islamic law should be the principal source of legislation covering all aspects of human life (this reference to sharia was already in the Egyptian constitution that existed before the revolution, and thus should not be seen as particularly alarming to secular forces). In the end, whether Egyptian laws and society become more "Islamic" will depend on how the principles of sharia are applied.

The Egyptian public is split on this question. According to a Gallup survey taken in February 2012, just months after the first parliamentary elections and before the presidential ones, 47 percent thought that "*sharia* must be the only source of legislation," while 46 percent believed "*sharia* must be a source of legislation, but not the only source."[11] Only 2 percent preferred no role for Islam's sacred principles (5 percent were unsure).

While much still needs to be unpacked regarding the Egyptian Muslim Brotherhood's stance on Islamic law, its inclusion of sharia as a principal source of legislation seems to reflect the wishes of most Egyptians. Yet this preference is more a reflection of Egyptian society's ambient conservatism than any active desire to establish a theocratic state. Even the Salafi Al-Nour Party accepted the reference in the Azhar document to sharia as the *principal* rather than the *only* source of legislation, although its chairman then, Abdel Ghaffour, told me the party did so reluctantly in order to achieve consensus. His statement could indicate a less than total commitment to a civil state, but it could also be seen as an indication that Islamist parties might moderate their views in exchange for political inclusion.

In contrast to the 2007 draft, the latest Brotherhood platform affirms that all citizens are equal and refuses any discrimination based on religion or gender. But it also includes a separate clause on women that seems to give them less than full rights. The language empowers women to have all the rights that "do not conflict with society's basic values, and which achieve a balance between a woman's rights and her duties."[12] It supports the right of non-Muslims to be subject to their own laws when it comes to personal status and religious worship, but adds that on all other issues the behavior of all citizens must conform to Islamic principles.

Despite its shortcomings, the platform is certainly an improvement over previous ones, and many consider it a moderation of the Brotherhood's earlier positions. For example, it not only explicitly acknowledges the Islamic principle of *shura* (consultation) but also adds that the best way to achieve shura is through democracy. The principle of the peaceful transfer of power is mentioned no less than four times, giving the impression that the Brotherhood would accept the will of the people. The platform also contains expressions like "parliamentary majority" and "political pluralism," suggesting that the Brotherhood does not believe in single party, or single-person, rule.

I met with Khairat Al-Shater, the Brotherhood's chief strategist and its charismatic candidate for the presidency in the 2012 elections before he was disqualified for having served a jail sentence under Mubarak. The meeting took place in Cairo in June 2012, when I was co-leading a Carter Center delegation to observe the Egyptian elections. Al-Shater reaffirmed his party's strong commitment to a civil state and to a peaceful alternation of power as called for in the Azhar document. "Our aim," he told me, "is to build a democratic and modern system that builds institutions, respects the rule of law, human rights, minority rights, and the independence of the judiciary, and is based on the most transparent criteria in modern states, all of which we lack now."

This brought us to an essential element in building a new Egypt: confronting the country's economic challenges, of which Al-Shater is unquestionably aware. "Our economic situation is in dire straits," he said. "Forty percent of Egyptians are under the poverty line, with twelve million Egyptians out of work. The economic situation must be at the top of the priorities of any president." He also said he did not believe that any single force can or should assume responsibility for the management of the country during the next ten years, a task that he believed must be assumed by a broad coalition. As of early 2013 the economic situation in Egypt has become even more dire, with foreign reserves dwindling fast and no indication that the Islamist government is addressing the situation effectively. Both the Islamists and the secular opposition have not displayed a serious will to work with each other. As a result, Al-Shater's assertion that a coalition must manage the country in the coming period has not materialized.

One of the oft-repeated criticisms of Islamist movements is that they lack detailed and realistic economic programs, and that their slogan, "Islam is the solution," is insufficient for addressing economic problems. It is true that economic issues did not rank high on the Brotherhood's agenda in the past, when the party was preoccupied mainly with its political identity and its relationship with the state. But with the Arab uprisings and the obvious need to focus on developing the economy, the FJP included a long economic section in its 2011 platform. It is heavy on rhetoric. While mentioning the main challenges facing the Egyptian economy—poverty, unemployment, corruption, the budget deficit, public debt, increasing inequality, a lack of social justice, erosion of basic services, and poor investment climate—the program lacks a holistic approach to dealing with them. It also fails to prioritize these issues and misses some key areas, like monetary policy.

The FJP's economic program shows the party's lack of experience in addressing these issues, which is not unexpected in a weak party system just emerging from autocratic rule. But the program deals inadequately with Egypt's dire economic challenges. It does not offer an alternative budget, for example, or detailed information on how to reallocate resources to meet its ambitious promises (such as increasing wages).[13] At the same time, it does not contain anything that should set off alarms for non-Islamists or the international community.

Nathan J. Brown and Amr Hamzawy note that the 2007 draft economic program revealed a preference for an interventionist state, while the FJP's political program called for a limited role of the state.[14] The current FJP economic program emphasizes private property and the role of the private sector, a market economy that values social justice under the framework of Islamic law, and the need for domestic and foreign investment. Critics of Islamist movements should not have major disagreements with the program as presented.

Clearly the Brotherhood's positions have developed over the years with nuances that defy the simplistic depiction of a movement bent on terror or holding inflexible ideological, political, and cultural views. While the Brotherhood is certainly not a democratic movement in the Jeffersonian sense, its position has evolved in the direction of established democratic norms. Its huge success in Egypt's first parliamentary elections moves it from an aspirant for a limited but meaningful role in the country's governance to a political leader. The question remains whether the Brotherhood will continue to modify its political and economic platforms and, if so, in which direction. Its participation in Egypt's political process has tended to moderate its views. And if its positions reflect the views of its supporters, its policies should continue to be moderate. According to recent polling, FJP supporters are just as likely as secular voters to support basic democratic rights, women's equality, and religious tolerance.[15]

Ennahda
The largest and most influential political Islamist movement in Tunisia, Ennahda is considered the most moderate of all Islamist movements in the Arab world. Founded in 1981 under the name "The Movement of the Islamic Tendency" and origi-

nally inspired by the Muslim Brotherhood in Egypt, it changed
its name to Ennahda in 1989. The radical positions it took at
its inception (it retroactively supported the takeover of the
U.S. embassy in Tehran in 1979) had grown more moderate by
the end of the 1980s. After gaining a plurality in the parliamentary elections of October 2011, Ennahda quickly demonstrated a willingness to work with secular parties.

The movement has had only one leader, Sheikh Rached
Al-Ghannouchi, whose extensive record of writing and interviews makes it easy to form a detailed view of the movement's
stated political, cultural, and economic positions.[16]

Ghannouchi's writings as well as Ennahda's program,
published in September 2011, indicate a significantly greater
commitment to political pluralism than that of the Egyptian
Muslim Brotherhood.[17] Ghannouchi defends freedom of expression for all citizens, including nonbelievers, and supports his case through quotes from the Qur'an, sayings of the
Prophet Muhammad, and positions of modern Muslim scholars. He also repeatedly refers in his writings to the Qur'anic
verse "No compulsion in religion." I asked him at a Carnegie
meeting in Washington, DC, in December 2011 whether that
principle stands at the macrocosmic level; in other words,
does he accept peaceful rotation of power?[18] Ghannouchi re-
plied that he does accept that principle. If, for example, the
Communist Party were to win an election in Tunisia, he said
his party would abide by the results. He challenged the "one-
way" reading of "no compulsion in religion," stating that if a
Muslim were to convert out of the religion, he or she would be
judged by God, not by man. In fact, Ghannouchi insisted that
religion has the potential to guarantee citizens' freedoms and
rights. In a March 2012 lecture on secularism he said: "There is
no value to any religious observance that is motivated through

coercion. It is of no use to turn those who are disobedient to God into hypocrites through the state's coercive tools. People are created free and while it is possible to have control over their external aspects, it is impossible to do so over their inner selves and convictions."[19] This principle is evident in the party's program, which supports guarantees for personal and public freedoms and freedom of belief and thought, as well as for the principles of pluralism and peaceful alternation of power.

At the Carnegie meeting, Ghannouchi said that the writing of the new Tunisian constitution should be a consensus-based process and should not be left to the majority. The constitution-writing process in Tunisia which ensued after that meeting has not been a smooth one, but Ghannouchi's claim was generally respected. After the 2011 election, Ennahda entered into a coalition government in which the prime minister came from its ranks, but the president of the republic and the president of the Constituent Assembly both came from secular, left-leaning parties: Congress for the Republic (CPR) and Ettakatol, respectively. The 2011 Ennahda platform explicitly states its commitment to a civil state based on a separation of powers, judicial independence, democracy, and equality among citizens.

Ennahda's stance on minority rights, however, is more complicated. In his earlier writings, Ghannouchi adopted many of the positions taken by the Muslim Brotherhood, maintaining that all citizens are equal, but that non-Muslims cannot assume the presidency, premiership, or leadership of the army. In December 2011, the Tunisian National Constituent Assembly announced the qualifications that a president must meet: Tunisian-born, Muslim, child of Tunisian parents, and at least thirty-five years old (Tunisia is 98 percent Muslim, so that qualification does not disqualify many people).[20]

The 2011 Ennahda program, however, highlights equality among citizens without qualifications. When I visited Tunisia in October 2011, as part of a National Democratic Institute delegation to observe the elections, Ennahda officials went out of their way to point out that their party lists included nonveiled women and that they will not tamper with the veil, which they said they regard as a personal choice. About half of Tunisian women are veiled, most citing "a religious mandate" as their reason for wearing the head scarf. Women in Tunisia are the least likely among Arab women to undertake this practice of adopting *hijab,* but most likely to do so for "identity" as opposed to religious reasons, suggesting that the hijab was sometimes a prerevolution protest symbol.[21]

Ennahda's officials stressed that of the forty-nine women elected to parliament in the 2011 vote, forty-three came from the ranks of Ennahda. The party has now even adopted the position that women can run for president.[22] Still, Ghannouchi has marked out a few religious exceptions where women do not have equal rights to men. No Islamist party in the Arab world, for instance, has accepted women as equals to men regarding inheritance, claiming that the religion is explicit about giving men twice the share that women receive.

Just as Ennahda's political platform is clearly more developed than that of the Freedom and Justice Party, its economic platform is likewise more comprehensive. It includes monetary and fiscal policy, and possible solutions for unemployment. But it still falls short of suggesting priorities. Still, like the FJP's platform, it holds no elements that should cause concern for Tunisians or the international community. It emphasizes a market-oriented approach coupled with a social responsibility to citizens—a model that has become mainstream around the world since the 2008 financial crisis. The program even calls for deeper relationships with the outside world, mentioning in particular the European Union, the United States, Canada, and Japan as targets for future economic partnerships. This pragmatic economic policy mirrors Ennahda's positions in other realms.

Ennahda is distinguished from other Islamic movements by the degree to which it insists on the need for constant renewal within Islam; by its willingness to work within the political context rather than always adhering to personal religious beliefs; and by its readiness to engage in coalition politics, at least in appearance, rather than attempting to rule alone. It displays particular sensitivity to the widespread fears in Tunisia that it might curb personal rights or impose a religious code of conduct on a society that prides itself on its secularism and cultural diversity.

Ennahda has attempted to calm skeptics through statements, if not always through action. Many secular forces accuse it of trying to dominate the constitution-writing process, and of being soft in its treatment of Salafi groups that have committed violent attacks against individuals accused of blasphemy. Some suggest Ennahda is using the Salafis and their extremist behavior as a scare tactic, much as the old autocracies did when they pointed at Islamist parties to make themselves appear to be the lesser of two evils.

Ennahda also faces a challenge from its own hard-line wing, some of whose leaders were elected to the party's leadership in its conference in July 2012. As a result, Ghannouchi, who had made clear his wish to retire from politics, was prevailed upon to stay on as chairman to prevent conflict within the party.

Tunisia has witnessed repeated paroxysms of tension. In the interior of the country, where the revolt kicked off, poorer and more disenfranchised Tunisians have been growing increasingly impatient with the continued lack of economic opportunities and the slow pace of reform. Meanwhile Salafi groups, which had long been sidelined by the secular authoritarian regime of Ben Ali, have now reclaimed their voices. Clashes have erupted, especially on university campuses, in art venues, and at media headquarters, over religious and nonreligious discourses. The transition to democracy, after a rather smooth start, has now encountered a rougher road.

The Party for Justice and Development

The Party for Justice and Development (PJD) in Morocco represents yet another example of a political Islamist party that has evolved since its founding to adopt moderation and advocate for pluralism. The party was part of Morocco's political system long before it won the November 2011 elections, and it is the leader of a coalition government today.

Established in the 1960s, the PJD has demonstrated its commitment to peaceful political participation and has legally taken part in Moroccan elections since 1997. It gradually increased its presence in parliament from 9 seats in 1997 (out of 325) to 46 in the 2007 elections, and then proceeded to win a plurality of 107 seats out of 395 in 2011. Under the constitution enacted in 2011, the PJD has the right to form the government. Like Ennahda, the party claims to be inspired by Turkey's Justice and Development Party (AKP).

Also like Ennahda and the Egyptian FJP, the PJD finds itself competing with a more radical party: Al Adl Wal Ihsan (Justice and Charity). Considered by some to be larger than the PJD, Al Adl Wal Ihsan is not a legally recognized party and has rejected participation in the political process. It has called for the transformation of Morocco into a republic or even a constitutional monarchy, as long as the king does not claim a religious role as commander of the faithful. Despite this competition, which occasionally pushes it to adopt conservative views to compete for Islamic votes, the PJD has always accepted the political structure of the Moroccan state and worked within it, thereby inviting criticism from part of its constituency.

In parliamentary debate, the PJD has focused less on questions of religious practice and instead has devoted much of its energy to political, social, and economic matters. For example, it supported the new civil code, known as *Al-Mudawanna*, which was passed by parliament in 2005 and significantly improved women's social status, giving Morocco one of the most advanced civil codes in the Arab world. Despite this, the PJD has been viewed with skepticism by many secular parties, and its record of dealing with such parties has been rather poor—at least until the November 2011 elections.[23] Today it is a leader of a coalition government that includes the Popular Movement and Istiqlal (both center-right parties), and the Party of Progress and Socialism (center-left)—as well as independents.

The PJD has expressed a commitment to pluralism and personal and minority rights throughout its history. In a communiqué issued in March 2011, it explicitly praised the "pluralistic nature of the Moroccan national identity," acknowledged the rights of the Amazigh minority, and called for this pluralistic identity to be recognized in the constitution—which it later was. The party went on to stress its belief in a government formed through free elections, specifically mentioning the important role that opposition parties play in governance.[24] PJD leaders have consistently declared that while they advocate an Islamic platform, their religious beliefs are a private matter and have no bearing on their policy choices.

The PJD has offered more details than either Ennahda or the FJP about how to tackle Morocco's economic challenges, although it similarly fails to prioritize programs or explain how to meet conflicting objectives. Like its Tunisian and Egyptian counterparts, the PJD has assured Moroccans it will take no measures to curb consumption or clothing preferences on the part of tourists. Indeed, all three Islamic parties have adopted similar moderate views on tourism and individual rights—a sign of maturity as well as an understanding of economic realities. The PJD seems aware of the need to keep Morocco's economy open to the outside world, in particular to the European and American markets, as these ties have been historically very important, politically as well as economically. In general, the program seems to emphasize the role of the private sector more than Tunisia's or Egypt's does.[25]

The Islamic Action Front

The Muslim Brotherhood in Jordan has had the longest history of political participation of any Arab Islamist group, albeit only informally until the formation of the Brotherhood's political wing, the Islamic Action Front (IAF), in 1992. Tolerated by the government since the 1950s, the Brotherhood enjoyed a tacit alliance with the regime, having opposed communism, leftist ideological parties, and Nasser's policies.

In 1989, after winning twenty-two out of eighty seats in Jordan's first general elections in three decades, the IAF formally entered the government with five cabinet positions. These included, among others, education, health, and social development, affirming the Brotherhood's preference for service delivery ministries that would buttress party support. The Islamists' performance in that role was mixed. Among other gaffes, its education minister caused an uproar when he banned parents from attending school performances by their children so as to avoid mixing the sexes. Jordanian society could not accept such a convoluted interpretation of religion, and after much public outcry the decision was reversed.

The Brotherhood's alliance with the regime came to an end when Jordan signed a peace agreement with Israel in 1994, a move that the Brotherhood and the IAF adamantly opposed. The tension with the regime has since deepened as a result of disagreements over two major policy issues: the war in Iraq and the war on terror. In both cases the IAF opposed a Jordanian official position that it considered too close to that of the United States.

Despite having participated in Jordanian political life for decades, IAF's current membership is growing more hardline than previous generations. The failure of the peace process and the prolonged Israeli occupation of the West Bank certainly provide one explanation. Particularly on the Palestinian issue, the IAF has moved much closer in its political views to its Palestinian counterpart, Hamas. In addition, the party's increasingly adversarial relationship with the regime on domestic issues such as corruption, political rights, and the role of the intelligence services over the past two decades has also contributed to its strong views. Younger IAF members appear less willing than their elders to accommodate the ruling system.

Notwithstanding its tensions with the regime, the IAF has historically been peaceful in Jordan. Even while supporting movements like Hamas and Hezbollah, it placed that support in the context of legitimate resistance against the Israeli occupation. Moreover, the regime and the IAF have never allowed the tension between them to reach a breaking point, and the overwhelming majority of Brotherhood leaders have called for serious political reform in Jordan under the king's leadership.

While it avoids specifics, the IAF party platform does refer to the "guarantee of political pluralism . . . and the enactment of legislative guarantees to assure it," and makes a specific commitment to religious freedom for all.[26] It supports women's rights to political participation, though not categorically, and it has had many internal disagreements about female participation.[27] The party has not articulated its stance on such principles as the peaceful rotation of power or guarantees for personal rights.

The IAF's economic program is very limited compared to the programs in Tunisia, Egypt and Morocco. It has offered a simplistic diagnosis of the country's main economic challenges, highlighting such issues as corruption, high commodity and fuel prices, a lack of social justice, and economic normalization with Israel. The fact that it is not in power in Jordan is another reason its political and economic positions have undergone the least evolution of the four Islamist parties under review.

Islamist parties that have won elections and are at least partners in government—in Tunisia, Morocco, and Egypt—have had to go beyond slogans and produce political and economic programs with real substance. The Islamist movements that are still in the opposition, as in Jordan, can postpone putting forward any specific measures until they have a viable shot at gaining power. Their programs, when they are written, are bound to alienate some of their constituencies who, for now, find in the Islamists' rhetoric echoes of their own complaints against the system.

Ideology or Results?

In every Arab country that held free elections in 2011 and 2012, Islamist parties made a strong showing. Their success has raised concerns that the Arab Spring might usher in theocracies rather than democracies. Years of survey research, however, paint a more complex and less pessimistic picture. On one hand, polls show that majorities in these countries endorse basic democratic principles and women's equality. On the other hand, the same studies find that majorities of Arab men and women favor some role for religious references in legislation, making any party with a strictly secular platform less likely to do well. Still, while most accept religious sources for law, the latest analysis also suggests that support for Islamists is more utilitarian than ideological and will likely depend on their performance in office. This popular pressure to deliver results will likely empower the Islamists' more pragmatic voices, as will the public's desire for freedom.

Contrary to the clash of civilizations theory, Arabs do not despise Western-style liberties; they desire them. Shortly after 9/11, Gallup asked Muslims around the world to describe what they admired most about the West.[28] The question was open-ended, and the most frequent responses included words like "freedom" and "democracy." People mentioned "fairness," "accountability of government to citizens," and "freedom" as among the qualities they most respected about Western societies.[29]

In 2005, when it seemed Ben Ali and Mubarak were securely entrenched in power, Gallup began asking people across the Arab world to imagine drafting a new constitution for a new nation. The question read, in part:

> Suppose that someday you were asked to help draft a new constitution for a new country. As I read you a list of possible provisions that might be included in a new constitution, would you tell me whether you would probably agree or not agree with the inclusion of each of these provisions?
>
> Freedom of speech—allowing all citizens to express their opinion on the political, social, and economic issues of the day.
>
> Freedom of religion—allowing all citizens to observe any religion of their choice and to practice freely.[30]

Three Arab countries that have undergone transitions or had recent elections were singled out: Egypt, Tunisia and Morocco. In the spring of 2012, when mass protests ended decades of one-party rule, large majorities in Egypt, Tunisia, and Morocco supported freedom of speech as a fundamental guarantee (Table 1). These results hardly reflect a public wishing to build a theocracy, and they do not represent a new trend. Similar percentages have favored this basic freedom every time Gallup has posed the question over the past seven years, suggesting that the views represent societal values rather than fleeting opinions born out of revolution fever. As Table 1 also shows, majorities in all three countries also support freedom of religion, albeit in smaller numbers than those who support free speech.

Majorities of men and women in these countries also support women's equal access to employment and legal pro-

Table 1. Polling response by country regarding support of freedom of speech and religion.

	Egypt	Tunisia	Morocco
Freedom of Speech—Allowing all citizens to express their opinion on the political, social, and economic issues of the day			
Agree	94%	95%	75%
Disagree	3%	2%	2%
Don't Know	3%	2%	22%
Freedom of Religion Allowing all citizens to observe any religion of their choice and to practice it freely			
Agree	70%	84%	49%
Disagree	25%	12%	25%
Don't Know	5%	3%	24%

Source: Gallup Center For Muslim Studies

tection. While majorities of both men and women favor legal gender equality and women's employment, men are consistently less likely than women to affirm these rights in all three countries. These gender differences are to be expected, but what is more striking is that the gap is greatest in Tunisia, often touted as the most progressive Arab country for women's rights. Tunisian men are twice as likely as their counterparts in Egypt, a far more religious population, to oppose legal gender equality. This finding suggests that a more secular culture does not necessarily lead to more feminist views (Table 2).

While they support these freedoms, most Arabs also want some role for sharia as a basis for legislation. To many Muslims, the term *sharia* means not necessarily a specific code but rather general principles. The percentage of those who prefer no role for Islamic references is in the single digits in the three countries. The main disagreement among these pub-

Table 2. Polling response by country and gender regarding support of women's rights.

	Egypt		Tunisia		Morocco	
	Men	Women	Men	Women	Men	Women
Women should have equal rights to men.						
Agree	79%	86%	59%	87%	72%	89%
Disagree	20%	12%	40%	12%	26%	7%
Women should be able to hold any job for which they are qualified.						
Agree	71%	89%	67%	89%	56%	82%
Disagree	29%	10%	31%	10%	42%	14%

Source: Gallup Center For Muslim Studies

lics concerns the extent to which lawmakers should rely on religious sources, with far more Egyptians (47 percent) than Tunisians (17 percent) favoring sharia as the "only source" of legislation. In Tunisia, the birthplace of the Arab Awakening, the majority want sharia to be among the sources—but not the only source—of law. Moroccans' views are somewhere in the middle (Table 3). As different as these societies are, few people in any of them envision a purely secular state, but most endorse basic democratic principles. These fluid, complex responses indicate that not many of those polled see a fundamental contradiction between the precepts of Islam and democratic principles.

While most people believe religious principles should inform government affairs, their support for Islamists is not necessarily ideological or unconditional. Like other publics, Arabs are motivated by complex influences, and their ballot box decisions are based on a number of variables. Support for public servants depends on how well their elected officials

Table 3. Polling response by country regarding support of sharia law.

	Egypt	Tunisia	Morocco
Sharia must be the only source of legislation.	47%	17%	37%
Sharia must be a source of legislation, but not the only source.	46%	58%	31%
Sharia should not be a source of legislation.	2%	7%	5%
Don't know	4%	15%	25%

Source: Gallup Center For Muslim Studies

appear to be delivering results. Egypt, as the most populous Arab country and the one with the strongest public support for sharia, provides a useful case study. Though Islamist parties won a decisive victory in the country's first postrevolution parliamentary elections, public opinion research shows a public focused more on results than on strict observance of religious law.

If most Egyptians were casting their votes for philosophical rather than practical reasons, we would expect the public's confidence in the religious-based political players to be fairly resilient, and their approval ratings steady. But the Muslim Brotherhood's support grew rapidly in the months before the election, jumping from 15 percent in March 2011 to 48 percent in December 2011—shortly before Egyptians went to the polls.[31] This increase suggests that weeks of effective campaigning, not years of philosophical followership, produced the Islamist parliamentary win.

When the new parliament took office, political squabbles and ineffective management of a turbulent transition quickly took their toll. After dominating the parliament for a few weeks, Islamists lost some of their luster. Support for the FJP dropped from 67 percent in February 2012 to 43 percent in April. The Salafi-affiliated Al-Nour Party suffered a similar fate, dropping from 40 percent support in February to 30 percent in April. This finding suggests that when Egyptians chose Islamists to represent them, they conditioned that support on performance.[32]

Egyptians are not prioritizing the government's role in social issues or religion's role in public life. Instead, whether they support Islamists or liberals, Egyptian voters' priorities are virtually indistinguishable from those of Americans: jobs, economic development, security, stability, and education.[33] The absence of sharp differences between the parties' voters on legal and social issues further demonstrates that support for a particular Egyptian political party is not driven by ideology, as it typically is in the United States. Supporters of the FJP look identical to those who endorse the liberal Free Egyptians Party when it comes to women's rights, interreligious tolerance, and basic constitutional freedoms.[34]

If the democratic process produces responsive governments, we would expect political participation to strengthen the more moderate voices within Islamist ranks. In numbers almost identical to those who support liberal political groups, the majority of Egyptian supporters of Islamist parties say they support women's rights to employment, equality before the law, and even women's rights to initiate divorce.[35] Strikingly, women's support for the FJP and the Al-Nour Party is virtually identical to that among men.[36] There was also no gender difference on whether "a parliament with a strong Muslim Brotherhood presence is a good thing for Egypt." Furthermore, across the Middle East, men's support for sharia is not linked to lower support for women's rights. Men's stated views of religious law have no correlation whatsoever to how they regard gender parity.

Instead, far more concrete factors drive men's support for women's equality. Among men, employment and a higher level of education correlate with support for women's rights. Across the Arab world, men's support for women's equal legal status and their right to hold any job for which they are qualified was positively linked to their own life satisfaction, employment, education, and other measures of economic and social development—not to their support for sharia.[37] This finding suggests that, in principle, economic challenges are a greater threat to women's rights than is public support for religious legislation.[38]

Demystifying the "Islamist Threat"

The threat of political Islam in the Arab world needs to be demystified. It is time to move beyond the stereotypical image often presented in the West. Islamists are neither the despots nor the democrats of the Arab world. The influence of political Islam has grown to a point where ignoring it or excluding it from the emerging political systems is futile. Most of these movements are peaceful, while the ones carrying arms have either been largely marginalized or are also moving toward peaceful political participation.

But there still remain questions about Islamist movements' belief in pluralism, peaceful rotation of power, and the rights of the individual, women, and minorities. We cannot yet say that these principles are really central to their political ideals. Of all the Islamist movements in the region, Ennahda has so far offered the most far-reaching, if not total, commitments to these principles.

Unquestionably there has been a gradual move away

from open claims of a monopoly on truth—and therefore power—and toward the acceptance of a more inclusive political framework. But it is also clear that Islamists are not fully there yet. Like many political parties, they may seek to abuse their dominant position through mechanisms that are camouflaged from the public. The secular groups in the Arab world, as well as the international community, are still fearful that whatever gesture the Islamists make toward pluralism and democracy today is simply a tactic to help them assume power. Once they gain the advantage, they may behave just like the Iranian regime. "One man, one vote, one time" still captures a widespread suspicion in the Arab world.

That fear is overblown. Political Islam is not monolithic, and it is fair to wonder whether Islamist parties are being held to a higher standard than other political groups in the region. After all, commitment to democracy and pluralism was hardly a defining feature of the old ruling elites, or even the secular opposition parties. The Nasserist, Baathist, nationalist, and monarchist regimes in the region have not been democrats. Women have been no more visible in secular political parties in the Arab world than in Islamist parties. As polling data shows, supporters of the FJP are as likely as those who favor the liberal Free Egyptian Party to endorse women's rights to legal equality and employment opportunities.[39]

During a visit to Egypt in June 2012, I noted that many secular leaders could accept the military's undemocratic practice of appropriating legislative and executive powers if that would check the growing influence of the Islamists. Emad Gad, vice president of the Egyptian Social Democratic Party, told me, "We do not live in a democratic society and we are in a transitional period; only the army can guarantee the principles of the constitution such as freedom and equality."[40] But the Brotherhood has also on several occasions tacitly supported the military, or at least failed to oppose its growing powers.[41]

Unlike the population of Iran, or that of Afghanistan in the early 1990s, Arab voters today are far more likely to hold their Islamist parties accountable for delivering better conditions. Polls clearly show that votes for the Islamists are not votes against democracy or for theocracy. Clear majorities in several Arab countries support democracy as the best option for their political systems—and show a clear understanding of what democracy means. This is best demonstrated by voter turnout rates exceeding 70 percent in Tunisia's first postuprising elections, and over 50 percent in Egypt. The majority of the population want a say in governmental matters. They also want jobs, better governance, and a more equitable distribution of resources.

The success of Hamas in the 2006 parliamentary elections in the West Bank and Gaza is particularly instructive in terms of the motivations that often inform voters' decisions. A poll conducted weeks after the elections clearly indicates that the vote for Hamas was more an anticorruption vote against Fatah, which until then had dominated the Palestinian National Authority, than a position on, say, how to deal with the Palestinian-Israeli conflict. The same poll showed that a majority of Palestinians wanted the Hamas government to start negotiations with Israel to resolve the Palestinian-Israeli conflict.[42] In other words, Hamas was elected on a vote that was far less an antipeace or an antidemocratic vote than it was an anticorruption, progovernance one.

The example of Hamas also illustrates what might happen when Islamists are brought into the political process. Hamas's popularity in Gaza has suffered a consistent decline from January 2006 through June 2011 as a result of governing methods that have not improved the quality of lives of Gaza's population (figure 1).

If Islamist movements choose the road of monopolizing power, the Arab world faces a turbulent future, but not necessarily one in which theocratic regimes will ultimately prevail. The protests in Egypt, Tunisia, and elsewhere have shown that secular groups are just as capable of putting people in the streets as Islamist groups. Given this recently discovered power of the street, populations are unlikely to stand idly by as secular autocracies are replaced by religious ones.

A crucial shift is taking place far from the cameras in Tahrir Square: there are rising expectations for delivering results and a rising belief that the public has the right to shape its own destiny. Whereas 81 percent of Egyptians said that they could "get ahead by working hard" in late 2010, this number jumped to 93 percent after the revolution and has remained stable since.[43] In a country once known for its people's quiet resignation, 90 percent now say that if there is a problem in their community, it is up to them to fix it. Egyptians believe that they have not only the responsibility but also the power to effect change; 55 percent believed this in September 2011, and 74 percent in December 2011.[44]

Most of the secular forces also said they will not sit idly by should anyone attempt to create anything other than a civil state. One can choose to doubt the Islamists' commitment to these principles, but the ongoing transformation of their movements into political parties has meant that they are abandoning the "holiness" associated with religion and entering a political field where they will be scrutinized just like everyone else, and where the ballot box is increasingly the ultimate decider. While the transformation to pluralistic norms among

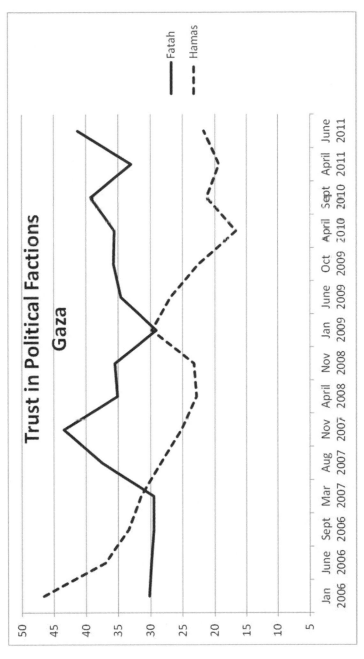

Figure 1: Trust in Political Factions in Gaza (based on poll data gathered from Jerusalem Media and Communications Centre [JMCC] from 2006 to 2011 [http://jmcc.org/poll.aspx])

Islamist and secular forces is not yet fully complete, it has already gained ground.

This chapter has covered the main Islamist parties that have won power in elections held in Egypt, Tunisia, and Morocco. But the rise of Salafi parties in these countries, some of which are militant and rigid, is a cause for concern. Although some of them have somewhat moderated their views as a result of participation in the political process, such as Al-Nour in Egypt, it is difficult to claim by any stretch of the imagination that they are likely ever to commit to genuine pluralism. Their narrow interpretation of Islam makes them believe in a society strictly governed by rules they think were adopted during Prophet Muhammad's day, and in their duty to force all of society to live by these rules. Whereas most of them did not believe until recently that they should enter the political fray, they have done so in countries such as Egypt and won a surprising 25 percent of the vote. In Tunisia, they were banned from participation in the October 2011 parliamentary elections precisely because of their lack of commitment to democratic norms (they were subsequently legalized in March of 2012). Some of them, particularly in Tunisia, have used violent means—a dangerous development.

Such illiberal, undemocratic, and violent parties need to be exposed not just by the secular forces, but also by the larger Islamist parties belonging to the Muslim Brotherhood and its offshoots considered by the Salafis to be too soft on Islamic principles. As indicated earlier, Al-Nour lost some popular support as a result of its performance in parliament (working for such issues as lowering the marriage age, for example, as opposed to solving economic problems, about which Egyptians are the most concerned). They have been financed by at least funds from private donors in Qatar and the Gulf, but it remains to be seen whether they are a transient or a permanent fixture of the political scene in emerging Arab systems, and whether the new constitutions being written would clearly prevent any party that does not believe in a peaceful rotation of power or in democratic norms from operating. If this is a battle for pluralism, it needs to be forged by both the secular and the moderate Islamist forces together—against exclusionist and violent Islamist parties.

4

Assessing What Has Changed

More than three years after the start of the uprisings, what judgment can one pass on this transformational change that has swept the Arab world? With four leaders already toppled—and counting—is the Arab world moving toward democracy? Or exchanging one set of autocratic rulers for another? Or reinforcing a political order that is fiercely resistant to change? The only safe judgment is that it is too soon to tell.

Beyond that, one's answer depends on the prism one uses. Many who insist on issuing a verdict after such a short time cannot help but see a process that is struggling: Islamists who are gaining power and threatening social norms; increasingly dire economic conditions; and, in some cases, as in Syria or Bahrain, sectarian strife that is threatening the cohesion of national communities. Some even feel nostalgic for the way the Arab world was, finding new wisdom in the argument of many Arab autocrats that the devil one knows is better than the devil one does not know. This is not an Arab Spring, many seem to feel, but an Arab inferno.

If we insist on a three-year window as our timeline for

evaluation, it is difficult to conclude otherwise. Populations are impatient and expect to reap immediate fruits from a revolution for which they have waited so long. The secular youth who started the revolutions in Tunisia and Egypt have helplessly watched as they have been pushed to the side while Islamists, with their long-standing structures and organizational experience, reap most of the political benefits. Dreams of an immediate improvement in economic opportunity have given way to a more frustrating reality. Dire economic conditions have been compounded with the immediate loss of investment and tourism, putting further strains on unemployment, budget deficits, and foreign currency reserves. And the dramatic rise of political Islam has caused Christians, secular Muslims, and others to worry about preserving their lifestyles.

But a three-year window is probably not the best prism through which to view the recent developments in the Arab world. The question over the long term is whether the present change, however uncertain and difficult, will lead to democratic societies. After all, the first "awakening" of the Arab world succeeded in getting rid of foreign autocratic rule, but it failed to produce pluralistic governments. Why should we expect the second awakening to do so? Can we detect signs that indicate whether countries of the Arab world are moving toward democracy and pluralism or away from them? Despite the despair and cynicism that has seeped into thinking about the Arab uprisings so far, the developments are not all negative.

Time Is No More an Infinite Commodity

Before the uprisings, almost all Arab regimes belonged to one category when it came to government reform. They all believed that "time is infinite," and they behaved as if they had all the time in the world to address the issue of governance and power sharing. None responded seriously to pressure to widen the decision-making circles. Since the revolts, however, Arab regimes can now be divided into two categories: the "time is limited" group—those that, because they still enjoy some legitimacy, have some time left to work seriously on political reform—and the "time is up" group, which comprises those that lost their legitimacy to rule.

Those whose time is up have basically surrendered—involuntarily of course—to the street, which took over the process of change. Some of these countries, like Egypt, Tunisia, Libya, and Yemen, have lost both their legitimacy and their authority, and their regimes have handed over power, mostly peacefully in Egypt and Tunisia's case, less so in Libya and Yemen's case, to new governments through electoral processes with varying degrees of orderly transition. Needless to say, the street is always better at starting change than at institutionalizing it in a smooth and constructive manner. These countries will go through different paces of transformation, depending on their level of development and political sophistication. The process will be bumpy—as it has been throughout human history—and many political and economic mistakes will be made before these countries set themselves on a course of sustainable stability. Their success in managing this transition will depend on the degree to which they embrace the values of pluralism, inclusion, and peaceful means, as well as on the degree to which they undergo processes that are holistic, inclusive, and measurable. These countries belong to the subcategory "rebuilding time." The first part of this chapter will look at two such countries in some detail: Tunisia and Egypt. But the transition has not always been smooth or peaceful, as

some countries have lost their legitimacy but not their authority, and they are desperately attempting to keep as much of the
status quo as possible. These belong to the "borrowed time"
subcategory, and we will look at two in particular, Syria and
Bahrain.

Ironically, the countries that have some time left for meaningful reform include most of the Arab monarchies, both the
poor and the rich. The latter group, comprising the monarchies of the Arab Gulf, mostly have not experienced the turmoil that countries like Egypt and Tunisia have. This is partly
because their financial resources have been sufficient to appease their citizens, and partly because their noncitizen migrant worker majorities do not wield the leverage to threaten
regimes. Members of that underclass can be deported if they
complain. Bahrain is a different case. Almost 70 percent of its
citizenry is Shiite and no longer satisfied with the paltry representation they receive at the hands of the Sunni minority that
rules the country.

Then there are the poor monarchies, Morocco and Jordan. The leaders of both countries enjoy legitimacy, and their
systems are more open than those of most other countries of
the Arab world. Popular protests in both countries in 2011 demanded significant changes. But the aspiration was for change
within the framework of the existing regime, rather than regime change, as the monarchy in both countries is seen as a
unifying institution. The regimes' responses to the uprisings
have been, as we will see, characterized by important similarities and differences. Both are attempting "reform from above,"
to stay ahead of the protests and avoid the fate of countries like
Egypt and Tunisia.

Genuine reform from above will no doubt be a gradual
process that does not introduce shocks to the system. It is eas-

ier said than done. There are not many successful examples
of leaders who have understood that the age of their absolute
power was over and that to keep power they had to share it,
and who have consequently ceded it voluntarily. While reform
from above might be preferable for the society as a whole,
leaders and the beneficiaries of the regime find its benefits difficult to visualize. The latter mainly see that they will lose the
special privileges they have gained in return for their loyalty.
It is often these groups—the retired officials, the intelligence
services, the regime's elders—who are most resistant to change
even when the ruler himself contemplates it.

Some distinct trends are emerging in all these countries
where transitions have started and where governments are attempting some semblance of a reform process in an effort to
ward off a more confrontational and revolutionary change.
Perhaps the first notable and rapidly evolving trend in countries such as Egypt, Tunisia, and Libya since early 2011 is the
conception—though not yet the real birth—of "third forces":
often disparate groups of people who are no longer satisfied
with the political duopoly of the old elites and the Islamist parties. Granted, Tunisia's Ennahda Party and the Muslim Brotherhood's Mohammad Morsi hold power today. But
while the resilience of status quo forces should not be un-
derestimated, it was third forces that, taken together, won a
majority of the votes in Tunisia, and third force presidential
candidates in Egypt (notably Hamdeen Sabahi, Abdel Munim
Abul-Foutouh, and Amr Moussa) who won around 50 percent of the vote to Morsi's 24.7 percent and Ahmad Shafiq's
23.6 percent.

These results for nonaligned forces are a sign that in
some parts of the Arab world, a new political orientation, articulated around new values, is attempting to break the cur-

rent mold and present itself as an alternative to the two dominant political forces. The realization that wide sectors of Arab publics need something different from what they have been offered since independence is setting in. The battle for pluralism has begun. It should have been waged a long time ago in the Arab world, to coincide with independence from foreign rule, but it has not truly broken out until now. The fact that it has started must be seen as a positive development, even if it is often obscured by the very turmoil it produces.

We must also parse the composition of these third forces along generational lines. The Arab world has witnessed in the past, and is witnessing now, secular forces belonging to an "old generation" that are attempting to challenge the traditional duopoly and offering themselves as alternatives. Most of these movements, however, revolve around individuals rather than around programs. They lack organizational capabilities and often temper their commitment to democracy when it conflicts with their short-term interests. These failings have discredited them to some degree among the newly active Arab populations, hampered their efforts to consolidate their forces, and cast doubt on their ability to build a critical mass of support.

There is, however, another generational third force in the making: youth groups who share the belief that a different discourse is needed, beyond autocratic governments and religious parties. These youth are more exposed to the outside world than their elders were and are more disenfranchised, and they strongly believe in the need to chart a course toward a society that respects pluralism, democracy, and human rights at all times, not only when it is expedient. But their disdain for personality cults has left them leaderless, and their youth means that they will need significant time before they can acquire the financial and organizational capabilities required for electoral success—particularly against entrenched old guards that are well heeled due to their capture of state resources (and sometimes funding from abroad). Youth itself provides an element of uncertainty, as people often change their views as they grow older—or become less passionate and more accommodating.

Developing the necessary electoral infrastructure to be a credible parliamentary force will require several more decades. Additional time will also have to pass before these forces are able to build the financial and organizational capacity that can transform wide social support into votes.[1] The youth in Egypt might feel that the revolution has been hijacked from them, and they may find themselves standing on the sidelines watching other forces, mostly Islamic, reap the benefits. But that frustration will quickly give way to the realization that the objectives of dignity, social justice, and freedom, while noble, are not enough to win elections if they are not coupled with detailed programs, hands-on work in the field, organizational capacity, and financial means.

That is the second trend that emerging third forces are quickly learning—the need to work on the ground. The Islamists have done this for decades, engaging in constituent politics, designing social programs and neighborhood activities, and working directly with people. Some secularists, in contrast, have spent their time alternating between elitist political theorizing and partisan smears against their political opponents. Rarely have they been seen interacting with ordinary people in poor neighborhoods. These habits have left many of them not only out of touch with the population and its concerns and culture, but also lacking sufficient networks on the ground to be successful. Third forces are only now absorbing the lesson that without these networks one cannot defend individual liberties and expand political and economic rights. Given that Arab regimes have often painted opposing political party members as treasonous, third forces have to redouble their efforts to persuade people to join and be active in party politics. At least the opportunity to do so is now open, and third forces, if they wish, will be able to build pluralism from the ground up, in the process strengthening their societies and their own support.

Yet a third trend is that Islamists began losing their aura of holiness the moment they entered the political arena. Whether religious or secular, conservative or radical, in or out of government, all those who enter the political fray can no longer invoke some unique higher wisdom. Electorates across the Arab world will now view all who aspire to lead them on an equal footing, as politicians. The field in Egypt, Tunisia, Morocco, and elsewhere is now open to all, and the people are the true source of authority, not purported divine guidance. Society has claimed the right to bring in or remove anyone from power. Religious parties can no longer claim a monopoly on faith or doctrine as a rationale for taking power, or indulge in pretensions of sainthood. Slogans such as "Islam is the solution" will not fly long if they do not bring people a better life.

By the same token, secularists cannot ban Islamists from politics on the pretext that they reject pluralism, particularly as secular forces have hardly shown a solid commitment to open politics. The "holiness" of both parties has lost credibility. Groups will be held accountable for their programs' success or failure in meeting citizens' needs.

A fourth trend is that the public will no longer accept sloganeering. While it may be easy to argue that citizens want bread before freedom, the economic reforms carried out under regimes like those of Mubarak or Ben Ali brought neither bread nor freedom to the average citizen. Having lost faith in a market liberalization that brought foreign investment and much wealth but did not lead to inclusive growth, Arab populations are no longer willing to tolerate unelected governments making unilateral decisions that further aggravate their own dire economic conditions, particularly given rising energy and food prices. Arab voters now expect economic policies to be made in consultation with those they affect, and to be closely monitored by strong, elected parliaments.

The economic and political factors that triggered the revolutions of the Arab Spring are closely linked: autocracy has led to corruption and economic injustice. Unemployment is the complaint most often cited, fueled by the youth bulge and made especially galling by the capture of public resources and opportunities by ruling cliques. Economic and political reform must therefore take place concurrently, promoted by institutional mechanisms of accountability that can check excesses and ensure at least some justice.

These four trends are still in their infancy. On their own, they do not guarantee a successful transition to democratic societies. They are easy to miss in the often messy transitions currently taking place. But they could determine the future of the Arab world.

How Is the Region Faring So Far?

Even though the transition to democracy must be measured in decades and not months, it is still possible to discern why some countries seem to be making better progress than others.

TUNISIA: THE INCLUSIVE TRANSITION

There is little doubt that the small country that started it all, Tunisia, is the one undergoing the smoothest transition. That is not to say that Tunisia's path is without serious difficulties, or that its progress is either linear or guaranteed.

At the outset the Tunisians established a Higher Committee for the Achievement of Revolutionary Objectives and Democratic Transition. This committee set the rules for the transition, including the establishment of political parties, a truly independent elections commission, and the sequencing of the transition (elections for a constituent assembly to draft a new constitution, then elections for a regular parliament). The principal problems are that the electoral results also determined the makeup of the executive, which has claimed broad authority, and the Constituent Assembly has been functioning as a de facto parliament, legislating and approving government budgets while also engaged in constitutional debates. Many Tunisians now say the technocratic interim cabinet that managed affairs in the immediate aftermath of Ben Ali's downfall should have been retained during the drafting of the constitution.

Still, because the rules of the political game were clearly laid down from the beginning, a majority of the Tunisian public sees the process as legitimate and credible. I was part of a team that monitored the Tunisian Constituent Assembly elections in October 2011. We met with representatives of all major political parties, and none offered major criticisms about the conduct of elections or the legitimacy of the process.

The Tunisians also set up the first truly independent body to monitor an election in the Arab world. Traditionally, this role falls on the ministry of interior, an organization that clearly has an interest in the outcome and generally impedes the fairness of elections in a variety of ways. One positive outcome of the uprisings is that conducting elections by independent commissions has become the recognized standard in Arab countries. In the wake of Tunisia's success, independent elections commissions have now been created in Morocco, Egypt, Libya, and Jordan.

The Tunisian process has also been aided by a neutral army, which acted as the protector of, not the interferer in, the transition. Unlike Egypt, where the army was the foundation of the old guard and often obstructed the transition to democracy, the Tunisian army stayed removed from politics, busying itself instead with matters of internal security and border patrols, rendered critical by the protracted crisis in neighboring Libya.

One important element in the Tunisian transition is the adoption of an election law, which consecrated a one-round voting system for the parliament based on proportional representation. That made it difficult for any party to gain an absolute majority. The biggest winner in the Tunisian elections, the Ennahda Party, obtained 89 out of 217 seats and ended up forming a coalition with two secular parties, Congress for the Republic (CPR) and Ettakatol. The president and speaker of the Constituent Assembly belong to these secular parties, respectively, while the prime minister was chosen from Ennahda's ranks. Some say those parties are so outnumbered by Ennahda as to constitute little more than a fig leaf. Still, their presence in a ruling coalition broadens the constituency of those in power.

Ennahda's apparently moderate outlook, as well as all parties' acknowledgement of the relatively secular nature of Tunisian society, have so far resulted in a governing system that does not appear to threaten personal rights or risk the imposition of cultural values on all of society. With respect to sharia law, the Constituent Assembly has agreed to retain the language found in the previous constitution declaring Tunisia a Muslim state—language that appears in most Arab constitutions today—but not to define sharia as the only source of law.

Tunisia's economy has not picked up as expected, however. A slower-than-expected recovery in tourism and foreign investment has brought predictable social tensions. The International Monetary Fund estimated unemployment at 19 percent in 2011, with youth unemployment at 42 percent. Growth was projected to reach only 2 percent in 2012, after the economy contracted by 2.2 percent in 2011 following the revolution. Tunisia's medium-term challenges, like that of Egypt, Jordan, and many other Arab countries, are job creation and addressing the structural issue of high youth unemployment.[2]

Another concern is the relative lack of attention that has been paid to the widespread economic crimes that characterized the Ben Ali regime—the acute corruption, bordering on state capture, that lit the revolution's fuse. Although the postelection cabinet includes a minister for governance and anticorruption, and another for transitional justice, there is little evidence of any effort to hold the guilty accountable and establish new operating norms in government bureaucracies, banks, and major businesses. If the old corrupt conditions are allowed to fester, and if Ennahda comes to some kind of arrangement with the leftover cadres of the Ben Ali regime, popular frustration in the coming years may fuel more unrest.

To the surprise of many, Salafis in Tunisia have proven to be a growing challenge. Banned from forming a political party until March 2012, they have engaged in violent protests against the state and some of its services, such as colleges and state-run media. Many secular liberals accuse Ennahda of engaging in double-talk, assuring the Tunisian and international communities of its moderate outlook but using Salafis and their bursts of violence to further Islamic influence in government institutions and the Tunisian way of life. At the very least, Tunisians secularists and liberals believe that Ennahda has failed to identify and punish Salafi groups or individuals who have violently attacked activists and intellectuals.[3]

An apparently contrary dynamic is the emergence of third forces after the revolution. These forces, still fragmented, are nonetheless trying to consolidate into a manageable number of parties that can pose a meaningful electoral challenge to the Islamist. It is easy to point to the internal tensions among them, and the external ones with the Islamists, as proof that these parties have not matured. Old-generation secularists in Tunisia, much like their counterparts around the Arab world, still view the Islamists with near-hysterical anxiety, seeing in their every move a hidden agenda to kill embryonic pluralism behind a veil of comforting rhetoric aimed at Western supporters. Ennahda, on the other hand, accuses the secular elements of being out of touch with Tunisian society and its inherent religiosity. Amid these tensions it is easy to miss the vibrant battle of ideas now occurring where previously none were allowed to emerge. As of this writing, a coalition of old-guard secular forces, Nida'a Tunis, is running almost neck and neck with Ennahda in polls, suggesting that the political field is leveling already.

On the other hand, the youth who started the revolution in Tunisia are now on the sidelines. The overwhelming majority of these third forces still belong to the old generation, with many young people acting as though they have some entitlement: because they started the revolution, its benefits should come to them without more work.

Still, as this first phase of the transition draws to a close, it is hard to deny that Tunisia will have held two parliamentary elections, created an independent and credible elections commission, experimented with coalition government, written a new constitution driven by popular consensus, kept its army neutral, and moved significantly away from repressive government. It will need more time to establish a proper system of checks and balances so that Islamists and secular forces accept that they can coexist, and so that alternative parties can emerge. So far, however, no Arab country can claim a more successful transition.

EGYPT: THE CONVOLUTED PROCESS

Egypt is a much larger and more complex country, with old-guard forces that arguably wielded more power—economic as well as coercive—than Tunisia's did. Its transition has been far messier. By the same token, Egypt's process will ultimately have more influence on the rest of the Arab world. Because Egypt is the most populous Arab country as well as the birthplace of the Muslim Brotherhood, what happens there will not stay in that country but will reverberate throughout the region, affecting the way the democratic process, the old guard, and Islamist movements evolve.

Although Egypt boasts the oldest parliamentary traditions and civil structures in the region, its democratic traditions have atrophied under sixty years of one-party rule, protected by a military establishment with huge economic privileges subject to no oversight, and by an internal security establishment that never flinched from abuse. Faced with an unexpected transition with no strong political parties other than the Islamists, and with heavy interference by the military, Egypt has been undergoing a convoluted, at times illogical process with sequencing that often has not made sense. The result has been a bumpy road, with many setbacks and much uncertainty.

Immediately following the fall of President Mubarak, Egyptians rallied behind the armed forces as the only possible guarantors of a fair transition. There were many reasons for this: the strength of the military, popular faith in the conscript army (whose rank and file hardly differed in background or upbringing from the youthful demonstrators), the credibility the army gained by refusing to fire on demonstrators, and sheer necessity. For many months, however, the military unilaterally appointed itself not only the "guarantor" of the revolution but Egypt's sole legislative and executive authority, with sweeping and unchecked policing powers. In March 2011, the Supreme Council of the Armed Forces (SCAF) administered a nationwide yes or no vote on draft constitutional amendments, written by a committee it appointed. Soon after the amendments' acceptance, the SCAF moved to introduce further amendments, this time with no public approval process. Although the military insists it has no desire to directly rule the country, it has consistently resisted civilian oversight of its actions and budget and has attempted to introduce legislation that would formalize its financial independence. During the second round of presidential voting, it moved to enact further constitutional amendments to allow it to appoint members of the Constituent Assembly, enforce martial law, and remain immune from oversight by government.

It is not surprising, therefore, that a transition process that was clearly not inclusive, and that lacked a logical plan, is facing so much difficulty. Some attribute the problems to the parliamentary dominance of two Islamist parties (the Muslim Brotherhood's Freedom and Justice Party won 43 percent of the parliamentary seats, and the Salafi Al-Nour Party won 21 percent). But the SCAF's consistent lack of transparency and occasional bold power plays led many Egyptians to blame it for the difficult transition, and to demand that it relinquish power to an elected civilian government.

After President Morsi retired senior SCAF members in August 2012, the question on many lips became whether he and his Muslim Brotherhood had simply taken the SCAF's place as the unchecked authoritarian—albeit elected—power. Although an election commission did monitor both the parliamentary and the presidential elections, it was a remnant of the Mubarak regime and hence seen as far less independent than its Tunisian counterpart.

In the end, neither religious nor secular parties shied away from collaborating with the SCAF when it suited their purposes. This revealed yet again that for the major players, political expediency still trumps commitment to democratic norms. The Muslim Brotherhood, for example, opted out of participating in a protest in November 2011 demanding the transfer of rule from military to civilian power. Many liberals viewed this decision as a move to appease the military at the expense of a truly democratic and civilian-led transition. Meanwhile, many liberal parties supported SCAF's proposed supra-constitutional principles, which would have limited the Islamist parties' influence over Egypt's government but granted the military additional powers. In June 2012, a few days after this proposal was made, presidential candidate Hamdeen Sabahi told me that even though he deeply distrusted the SCAF, he was not particularly unhappy about its clearly undemocratic move to give itself sweeping powers. His fear of an Islamic theocracy trumped his fear of military rule. This may be evidence that the "deep state"—a term Egyptians use to describe the nation's deeply entrenched structures and power centers—has not been greatly affected by the departure of Mubarak, and that the country has a long way to go before it undergoes a true revolution. It also shows that democratic norms do not emerge anywhere overnight.

The dominance of the bipolar forces—the military and the Islamists—was abundantly clear when I visited Egypt in June 2012 to observe the second round of the presidential elections. Despite some third force candidates who contested the first round with considerable public support, in the end the state machinery and the Islamists' organizational experience managed to catapult two uncharismatic, unimpressive candidates into the lead. It was not really those two individuals—Ahmad Shafiq, the prime minister in Mubarak's last days of rule, and Mohammad Morsi, put forward by the FJP after its preferred candidate, Khairat Al-Shater, was disqualified by the election commission—in the ring, but the machinery of the state pitted against that of the "Ikhwan" (Arabic for "The Brotherhood"). In the end, the latter won, partly because many people who would have preferred not to vote for the Islamists could not bring themselves to cast a ballot for a regime they had just fought to depose. They either voted for the Islamist reluctantly, did not vote, or (as 3.2 percent did) deliberately invalidated their vote by going to the polls and spoiling their voting papers.

While it is heartening that third forces in Egypt have attempted to break the old bipolar monopoly, all of them are built more around personalities than around programs, with leaders who are more liberal than democratic. Many secular figures, like Sabahi, appeared to accept from the Islamists the same authoritarian practices they deplore. Further, most of these secular leaders were unwilling to join forces to create a consolidated front that would have a fighting chance against the state's and the Islamists' formidable political machines.

These old-generation secular leaders seemed more focused on maximizing their own political profile than on establishing pluralism as a founding principle of the new Egyptian order. Like the former authoritarian clique, they seemed to regard such a commitment as premature.

The new generation in Egypt seems more promising. In several meetings with some of its representatives—both Islamist and secular—I thought their commitment to democracy appeared much stronger. Their command of politics and their analysis of the current situation were both deep and impressive. They were clearly more worldly than their elders and more committed to a discourse that is both secular and democratic. "A cultural war between Islamists and secularists is unhelpful to the cause of democracy in the long run," Hossam Bahgat, executive director of the Egyptian Initiative for Personal Rights and one of the savviest young Egyptians I met, told me. "We want to defend everybody's right to operate." Groups like his, unfortunately, have lacked the organizational capability and the financial means to reach beyond their small circles to the whole country. It is thus difficult to speak of a formidable third force yet. But with 32 percent of Egyptians under fifteen years of age, the future holds promise for the evolution of a pluralistic culture.

One of the positive developments in the Egyptian transition is the endorsement by almost all major political forces in the country—including the Muslim Brotherhood and the Salafi Al-Nour Party—of a document drafted by Al-Azhar, the oldest and most respected institution of Islamic learning in the Arab world. Released in June 2011, it was a semiconstitutional declaration committing all the major forces in the country to a civil, democratic state. It is instructive to examine some of its language verbatim, as its principles, which largely align with those of a modern democratic state, were expected to be endorsed in the new Egyptian constitution.

So hereby we, the meeting participants, agreed on the following principles in determining the features of the Islamic reference represented in several issues extracted from the religious texts which are definite and accurate and they are:

First: Al-Azhar supports establishing a modern and democratic state according to a constitution upon which Egyptians agreed and which separates between the state authorities and its governing legal institutions. Such a constitution should establish rules, guarantee the rights and the duties of all the citizens equally and give the legislative power to the people's representatives in accordance with the true Islamic principles. Islamic states[,] whether culturally or historically[,] differ from other states which rule by oppressing its people and from which we humans [have suffered] a lot in the past. Islamic states let people manage their societies and choose their ways and techniques to achieve their interests provided that the Islamic jurisprudence is the main source for the legislation in a way that guarantees to other divine religions' followers the right to appeal to their religions in their personal issues.

Second: Al-Azhar embraces [a] democracy based on free and direct voting which represents the modern formula to achieve the Islamic precepts of *shura* (consultation). Islamic precepts include pluralism, rotation of power, determining specializations, monitoring performance, seeking people's public interests in all legislations and decisions, ruling the state in accordance with its laws, tracking corruptions and ensuring the accountability of all people.

Third: the commitment to freedom of thought and opinions with a full respect of human, women and children's rights, to multi-pluralism, full respect of divine religions and to consider citizenship as the basis of responsibility in the society.

Fourth: full respect of counter opinions and the manner of dialogue, avoid[ing] labeling people as believers or traitors, making use of religion to disunite citizens and pit them against each other and consider acts of instigating religious discrimination, sectarianism and/or racism as crimes against the state; Al-Azhar supports dialogue and mutual respect between citizens based on equality in terms of rights and duties.

Fifth: the commitment to all international conventions, resolutions and achievements consists with the tolerant Arab and Islamic culture along with the long experience of Egyptians throughout the ages and the good examples that Egyptians set of peaceful co-existence and seeking the interests of all humanity.

Sixth: Al-Azhar is committed to preserve the dignity of Egyptians, to defend their national pride, to protect and fully respect the places of worships of the followers of the three heavenly religions, to safeguard the free and unrestricted practices of all religious rites. Al-Azhar also is keen on uphold-

ing freedom of artistic and literary expression and
creativity within the context of our fixed cultural
values.[4]

Most people look at what is happening in Egypt as a
fight over the nature of Egyptian society—whether it becomes
a theocratic state or not. The broad consensus in support of
the Al-Azhar document suggests that Egyptians, in the main,
agree on the nature of the intended new state. This view was
supported in interviews I conducted with Islamist figures such
as Ahmad Al-Tayyeb, the Grand Imam of Al-Azhar; Imad
Abdel Ghaffour, chairman of the Salafi party Al-Nour, and
Khairat Al-Shater, a leading FJP figure and their chief strategist. "There is no concern about the reversal of the civil nature
of the Egyptian State," Sheikh Al-Tayyeb told me. "A theocratic
state is not accepted by wide sectors of Egyptian society." Even
the Salafi Abdel Ghaffour informed me that a theocratic state
"only exists in the Shiite doctrine. . . . We accept political pluralism. Having accepted the political rules of the game, we
have to accept the results, even if they are not in our favor."[5]

One cannot discount the possibility that these comments
might be less than sincere, and that these positions might be
reversed when their proponents gain power. But one should
not dismiss them outright either, particularly when they are
given such a public endorsement in the Al-Azhar document.

A group of young activists I met with in Cairo told me
that the real fight in the constitution writing process is not
about minority or individual rights, all of which seem to enjoy
wide consensus, at least as far as the text of the document is
concerned. Rather, it is over the mechanisms for guaranteeing
those rights: the nature of the political system and the divi-
sion of power between the president and parliament. Islamists

want a largely parliamentary system with limited powers for the president, as it is easier for them to win a plurality in parliament than to win the presidency, while many secular elements prefer a mixed system in which the president has real powers, albeit less than those enjoyed by Mubarak. Another contentious point had been the role of the army and how much power it will retain—an issue that will surely be affected by Morsi's sacking of SCAF senior officers in August 2012. Finally, many activist youth believe the new constitution should address the state's role in guaranteeing minimal "social justice"—taking care of the most disenfranchised in society. They expressed great frustration that these important social issues are being ignored.

The economy will play a major role in determining the course of the transition. The success or failure of the new Islamist-led government might largely depend on how well it addresses the dire economic conditions facing the country. FJP leaders are aware of this. Khairat Al-Shater explained to me at length his party's plan to create jobs, attract investment, and develop a new educational framework. He seemed aware of what was at stake for his party. "Egypt's challenges," he told me, "cannot be addressed by any one political force alone. Egypt must be ruled by a broad coalition in the next five to ten years."

Once again, it is not the Islamists' economic policies that are of highest concern to most economists, but rather their lack of experience in managing the economy, as well as the need for political stability. As we saw in chapter 3, the economic programs of Islamists in Egypt, Tunisia, and Morocco are all market oriented and contain no radical breaks with policies of the regimes they replaced. "The Brotherhood might be more liberal economically than Ahmad Shafiq," an Egyptian economist (who wished not to be named) told me. "We have all the elements for a recovery, provided we have political stability."

Ahmad Galal, head of the Economic Research Forum, one of the region's most prestigious economic think tanks, agreed. "We have a diversified economy that structurally has the potential to rebound once we have political stability," he said. He also reminded me that as difficult as the state of the economy is today, it is not as bad as it was in the late eighties, when the budget deficit reached 20 percent of GDP (it was 10 percent in 2012) and inflation reached 20 percent, also double what it is today. Galal was more concerned with the Islamists' lack of experience managing an economy than with their outlook, pointing out the difference between delivering services and managing an economy. "Delivering retail style is different from fixing systems nationwide," he observed. Still, he claimed to be more optimistic than most. "The country was at a low, stagnant level of equilibrium, but the new equilibrium in a few years could be at a much higher level and more balanced if things are done right on the political and economic fronts." What worried Galal most was the future of the social agenda. The old regime had failed to deliver on "the social agenda (taking care of the less privileged groups in society), not on the growth agenda (achieving healthy overall growth rates)." This confirms what others have pointed out: growth that is not inclusive will not solve the country's economic problems.

The economic challenge in Egypt is not a matter of conflicting economic ideologies (the differences between political factions are not huge) but about approaches to economic justice. Past governments used state machinery to enrich a very small segment of the society with absolute impunity. There is widespread agreement that future governments must find the ability to create jobs, attract investment, and redirect subsidies on basic commodities, targeting them to care for the less privileged. There is less agreement on the specific measures that will best address these needs. Egypt will find that no unelected government from now on can continue to take unpopular but needed economic measures without the consent of the governed through the ballot box. When seen from that angle, dire economic conditions might actually prove helpful to political reform.

However, the economic situation continues to worsen. Foreign reserves have decreased from about $33 billion before the revolution to about $13 billion in early 2013, hardly enough for two months of imports. I found the country in a somber mood during a visit I made in February 2013. Political parties were still busy battling among themselves and not doing much about the pending economic cliff. Egypt still has a long way to go before it achieves political and economic stability.

As indicated above, not all countries in the time-is-up group have started the rebuilding process. Others, like Syria and Bahrain, have regimes that are still in power but no longer command their earlier legitimacy. These two countries share many similarities. Both have diverse populations but are governed by minority regimes, and hence their strife has sectarian overtones; in addition, both have been affected by powerful outside actors.

BAHRAIN: SOLUTION MUST BE POLITICAL, NOT SECURITY-BASED

At 296 square miles, Bahrain is the smallest Arab country. But it is unique in more than one way when viewed through the lens of the Arab Awakenings. Bahrain is only one of two

Arab countries (the other is Syria) ruled by a minority regime: 70 percent of the population is Shiite, heavily unrepresented in government and parliament, and is ruled by a Sunni royal family. It is also the first Arab Gulf country to discover oil, although it has a limited production of about forty thousand barrels a day and its supply is not expected to last beyond the next fifteen years. Bahrain was the first "rich" Arab monarchy to experience serious unrest. To its west lies Saudi Arabia, its big neighbor that provides it with significant economic and political help, and with which Bahrain has aligned much of its foreign policy. To its east lies Iran, with which 70 percent of Bahrainis are co-religionists, but whose policies are fundamentally at odds with those of their country.

The new emir of Bahrain (later king), Hamad Bin Issa Al-Khalifah, realized that the status quo was not sustainable once he assumed the throne after the death of his father, Sheikh Issa Bin Salman Al-Khalifah. In 2001 he introduced a new charter that called for the creation of a constitutional monarchy, with a two-chamber house of parliament that included an elected lower house. By 2002, however, most of the promised reforms stalled, and the opposition, mainly Shiite but also including Sunnis, complained that parliament was more of a "debating society" than one with real legislative and oversight powers.[6]

The young became increasingly frustrated that reform was largely cosmetic and were particularly upset that the main Shiite opposition political force, Al-Wifaq, could not effect much political change after it entered parliament in 2006.

On February 14, 2011, a mere two months after the Arab uprisings started in Tunisia, and then spread to Egypt, thousands of young activists went into the street, with demands that were largely nonsectarian—focusing on corruption, housing shortages, political reforms, and human rights, as well as on ending discrimination against Shiites. Although the king and his reform-minded son Crown Prince Salman initiated discussions with the leaders of the opposition, these did not amount to much. Nearly a hundred people lost their lives in the first two months of demonstrations, and the king declared martial law after more than a hundred thousand (in a population of 1.3 million) protesters took to the street, and called for Saudi troops to enter the kingdom, which they did on March 14, 2011.

Bahrain is another example of a small country with leaders who were relatively open-minded, one in which reform from above could work, particularly as even most of the Shiite opposition was not calling for regime change, but rather for fair representation and equal rights. Yet, three years later, the country is stuck; new security and financial measures temporarily won over the opposition, but the leaders have not moved much to put in place a more stable and sustainable solution. Some of the reasons for this state of affairs are internal, with the real political power being in the hands of the hard-liners, represented by the prime minister, uncle of the current king, who has been in power for forty-plus years—and who refuses to relinquish any of it. But Bahrain has also been largely affected by the real or perceived intervention of its two big neighbors in its domestic affairs.

The Saudis, themselves a monarchy ruled by a Sunni royal family with sweeping powers, can ill afford to have at its doorstep another Gulf country with plans for a constitutional monarchy and, worse yet from the Saudis' point of view, one that might be ruled by the Shiites. To the Saudis, this would both embolden their own Shiite population of about 10 percent, as well as give Iran a foothold in their backyard. Consequently, the Saudis opposed any moves by the king and crown prince of Bahrain for meaningful political reform, and used their economic leverage and security measures to nip any reform movement in the bud.

Iran's intervention in the Bahrain crisis is a matter of contention. The Bahrain Independent Commission of Inquiry, set up by the king to investigate the uprisings, submitted its report in November 2011 and concluded there was no evidence of any Iranian role in the protests, even if it also opined that the Iranians made use of the situation for propaganda purposes.

Is the strife in Bahrain a sectarian one, then? The Sunni-Shiite divide in the region has long been the subject of debate among scholars and politicians alike. In recent decades the Khomeini revolution in Iran, the war on Iraq that led to a Shiite-controlled government, and the rise of Hezbollah in Lebanon have all fueled this debate, painting the picture as a religious struggle between Islam's two major sects.

But while such struggles have sectarian overtones, the truth is more nuanced. The opposition in Bahrain has legitimate political demands for equal rights and political freedoms, as well as economic ones, for better housing and living conditions. The Shiite minority in Saudi Arabia has long been marginalized, politically and economically. It is easy for governments to paint this as an attempt by the Shiites to assume political dominance, or to claim they are puppets of the Iranian regime. But there is much truth to the fact that most demands by Shiites in Bahrain and Saudi Arabia are not about a particular religious doctrine, but for treatment as equal citizens. Meeting these demands would go a long way in bridging whatever religious gaps exist between the two sects. As Frederic Wehrey of the Middle East Program at the Carnegie Endowment for International Peace accurately described it, "The Shi'a of Bahrain and Saudi Arabia rose up in solidarity with the crowds of Tahrir Roundabout and Tunis rather than their co-religionists in Najaf, Qom, or southern Beirut."[7]

Bahrain is in many ways a victim of its own internal royal family politics, the lack of a political will to institute meaningful reform-from-above process, and heavy outside influence from its more powerful neighbors. But it is clear that security and financial measures cannot solve the country's structural problems. Without a political solution that treats all its citizens as equals, probably under a constitutional monarchy, it is living on borrowed time.

SYRIA: AN EXISTENTIAL STRUGGLE

In a January 2011 interview with the *Wall Street Journal* in response to the uprisings in Tunisia and Egypt, Syrian president Bashar Al-Assad said, "We have more difficult circumstances than most of the Arab countries, but in spite of that Syria is stable. Why? Because you have to be very closely linked to the beliefs of the people."[8]

Less than three weeks later, hundreds of Syrians held a spontaneous protest in Damascus's Souq Al-Hamidiyeh over the beating of a local shop owner by the police. On March 6, a number of young boys were arrested in Daraa, a southern Syrian city on the Jordanian border, for writing on city walls "The people want to overthrow the regime." A "Syrian Day of Rage" followed on March 15, during which some one thousand protesters asked for the young boys' release. On March 18, 2011, protests broke out all across Syria in Daraa, Homs, Banyas, Qamishli, and Deir Al-Zawr.

Typical of an out-of-touch regime, Assad waited nearly a month, until April 16, to give his first speech to the Syrian people in response to the uprisings. In his remarks he claimed that the protests were the result of a conspiracy directed at Syria by the international community, which he said sought to target the country due to its status as a "resistance state" against Israel.

Two years later, as of the writing of this book, the Syrian crisis lingers on. More than ninety thousand have been killed, a million-plus refugees are huddled in camps or donated lodgings, or taken in by relatives in neighboring Jordan, Lebanon, Turkey, or Iraq, and another three million are internally displaced. Despite the regime's brutal response, which has been responsible for much of this suffering and the death and torture of thousands of people, Syrians kept their revolution overwhelmingly peaceful for months before the spontaneous uprising evolved into an armed rebellion. By late 2011 significant numbers of defectors from the regime's armed forces joined with Syrian volunteers to organize efforts for military action against the regime.

Syria's population is remarkably diverse, both ethnically and religiously, for its small size. About 70 percent of the population are Sunnis, 12 percent Alawites—an offshoot of Shi'ism that is considered heretical by many Muslims—5 percent Druze (another monotheistic breakaway from Shi'ism), and 12 percent Christians. In addition, 9 percent of the Syrian population are Kurds, mostly Sunnis by religion but ethnically not Arab. Each of these groups has close ethnic and religious ties to communities in neighboring states—in particular Turkey, Iraq, and Lebanon.

Since Bashar Assad's father came to power in 1971, Syria has been governed by a regime led by members of the tiny Alawite minority, which promoted itself as secular but ensured the political domination of an Alawite elite allied with some key Sunni businessmen over all other Syrians. Assad and his father before him embraced the strong anti-Western narrative favored by Tehran and sought to burnish their credentials with public opinion by positioning Syria as a frontline state against Israel's occupation of Palestine.

As the Syrian revolution turned violent, it inevitably could not remain a domestic affair for long. As the revolution became militarized, outside forces started interfering. Sunni countries such as Turkey, Saudi Arabia, and Qatar began providing financial and material support for Sunni groups, including those promoting radical Islamic ideologies, while Iran and Russia have been backing the regime. The ensuing radicalization—"Islamization"—and sectarianization of the conflict is an extremely troublesome development. An uprising over political grievances has increasingly taken on religious overtones, to the point that almost all other non-Sunni communities (Christians, Druze, and Alawites) that have themselves suffered political repression under the regime nevertheless support it for fear of the advent of a Sunni alternative that might be exclusionist and vengeful toward minorities. The opposition, whose attempt to display a united front against the regime went through many iterations over the first two years of the revolution, has neither adequately achieved that objective nor provided minorities with convincing guarantees that they could enjoy a safe future in a post-Assad Syria. Meanwhile, two years into the revolution the country was half-destroyed. According to an unpublished UN study, as a result of the relentless fighting and destruction, particularly in urban areas, Syria has already lost an estimated 35 percent of its preconflict GDP and is on a path to lose as much as 58 percent—an unimaginable number—by 2015 if the destruction continues unabated.

As of late 2013, there was no end in sight for the Syria

conflict. A military deadlock between the two sides has per-
sisted, as neither has been capable of dealing a final blow to the
other. The regime is no longer behaving as a state that provides
structure or services to its citizens, but as a loyalists' militia
concerned only with survival and willing to employ all instruments to that end—airpower, tanks, surface-to-air missiles—
even at the expense of destroying the institutional, architec-
tural, and human fabric of the country.

For its part, the international community has been locked
in a debate over whether or how to intervene as the humanitarian crisis grows more acute daily. While the United Nations
Security Council agreed to a cease-fire plan in June 2012 envisioned by the UN and Arab League envoy Kofi Annan, it had
no chance of being implemented because the United States
and Russia disagreed on its interpretation from the moment it
was adopted. The so-called Geneva plan called for a complete
cease-fire and then a negotiated political solution, including
an inclusive, Syrian-led political process to start a transition
to a new government of national unity. Neither side, however,
is interested in sitting down with the other. The opposition
has not accepted any plan that does not explicitly call for the
ouster of Assad, while the regime views this conflict as an all-
out existential war for its physical survival and is not willing to
consider fundamental dismantling of the Baath apparatus.

What has transpired in Syria has been unprecedented
among the Arab uprisings that have erupted so far. Whereas
outside interventions in Libya and Bahrain have been successful in ending the military conflicts there (in favor of transition
in Libya and stagnation in Bahrain), outside involvement in
Syria has been on both sides of the conflict and has served to
increase the violence rather than diminish it, as different outside forces funnel equipment and support to their proxies in

the country. The nonhomogenous nature of Syrian society has also resulted in an escalation of intergroup tensions, conflict, and fears that have obstructed an early resolution to the conflict and reinforced the regime's sectarian narrative.

Yet despite these brakes on transformation, a scenario in which Assad would remain in power seems extremely difficult to imagine. He has lost legitimacy among a large majority of the population and has shown unusual brutality in killing and stampeding people out of their homes and villages, and destroying the infrastructure of his own country. But the conflict might persist for some time, leading to one of a number of potential developments, including the fragmentation and the balkanization of the Syrian state. The stable and pluralistic Syria imagined by those who first demonstrated in support of a handful of young protesters back in 2011 appears to be a goal that has receded far from the horizon. Whereas Egypt and Tunisia, helped by their homogenous societies and relatively quick and peaceful demonstrations, might still take decades to establish the foundations of a functioning democracy, Syria's foundations will have a much longer and more painful trajectory. The longer the destruction continues, the more uncertainty that this goal can be achieved in the foreseeable future.

MOROCCO: REFORM FROM ABOVE

As I write this, Morocco's monarchy has succeeded in staying ahead of the street by acting quickly to address at least some of the basic demands of its protesters, who have sometimes numbered in the hundreds of thousands. For now it has defused the protests.

Morocco's political culture includes paradoxical elements. The country boasts one of the oldest traditions of party-based parliaments in the Arab world. Yet it has a monarch with broad powers and extensive business interests, and its parliament has historically been ineffective in wielding power independent of the king. Morocco's Islamist political party, the Party for Justice and Development (PJD), has always acted as loyal opposition, working within the system and acknowledging the king as "commander of the faithful." Al Adl Wal Ihsan, a rival and probably the larger Islamist group, does not acknowledge the king's legitimacy and refuses to participate in elections. Morocco had a record of serious human rights abuses under King Hassan II, yet the same monarch moved in the 1990s to open up the system, including appointing an opposition party to lead the government.

King Muhammad VI acceded to the throne in 2000, and early in his tenure made a number of significant reforms—although none that would significantly affect his powers. He established an Equity and Reconciliation Committee in 2004 to uncover human rights abuses committed under his father, rehabilitate the victims, and compensate them for the abuses they suffered at the hands of the state (though the committee's work did not extend to his own rule). In addition, the 2004 Family Code, *Al-Mudawanna,* passed by parliament with the approval of the PJD, went far in improving the status of women in the country. In another first in the Arab world, and a rare triumph for diversity, the king started to improve the legal status of the Amazigh (previously known as Berbers) until their rights and language could be fully recognized in the new 2011 constitution.[9]

Muhammad VI moved more swiftly than any other Arab leader to try to stay ahead of the street after mass protests began in early 2011. Supported by *al-makhzan,* a coterie of political and business elites close to the crown, the king appointed a committee to amend the constitution, put it to a referendum, and held elections in November of 2011. He then appointed as prime minister the secretary-general of the PJD, which had won the plurality in the elections. Even though the king gave away very little actual power—other than permitting the party that wins a plurality of votes to form the government—the symbolism was powerful enough to dissipate the protest movement. This reduction in tension perhaps shows how reasonable Arab publics can be even when faced with limited reforms, if they believe there is a political will to make further progress.

The process of amending the constitution was hardly inclusive. Although it sometimes consulted with political parties and civil society, the committee was formed from proregime figures appointed by the king, and the draft was put to an up-or-down popular vote, with no room for discussion or public input. Still, the novel sight of a government headed by an Islamist, not chosen by the king, lent at least some credibility to the process.

Morocco's trajectory will partly depend on whether the cabinet exercises to the fullest the authority given to it by the new constitution. Its declared objective of fighting corruption will put it at loggerheads with the palace elite. The PJD publicly presents itself as "a third way" in Morocco, a force that belongs neither to the old ruling elite or to hard-line, ideological Islamic groups, but this claim is, to put it most charitably, premature. Judging from the cabinet's performance so far, it seems to be not so much independent as co-opted by the palace. Not only is it unwilling to confront serious issues such as corruption, it has deferred to the palace even in areas where the new constitution gives it independent authority.[10]

Meanwhile, as in Egypt, the youth who started the protests have watched the Islamists reap much of the benefits. The best-known youth movement in Morocco, February 20 (named after the date in 2011 on which hundreds of thousands of mostly young people spontaneously took to the streets demanding change), lost much of its momentum and largely dissipated once the hard-line Islamist party, Al Adl Wal Ihsan, withdrew its support in December 2011. Still, if we are looking for a true third force to emerge, it is more likely to come from the new generation than from an Islamist party that may be too cozy with the old guard to deliver on governance effectively.

Morocco has taken important steps toward reform, both before and since the Arab uprisings. But the jury is still out on whether its effort at reform from above can succeed. The answer will largely depend on whether the reforms continue. That will take more than shrewd moves by the king and the makhzan to stay ahead of the street. It will require a genuine commitment to a process that would lead to true power sharing.

JORDAN: THE SQUANDERED CHANCE

In many ways, Jordan is the model of what a second Arab Awakening could have looked like. But the potential has not been realized yet. Ruled by a monarchy that is accepted as legitimate by the overwhelming majority of the population—and necessary as a unifying force for the country's different ethnic groups—Jordan started the rule of King Abdullah II in 1999 with much hope. The new king was thirty-eight years old and eager to lead a modern country that would be a model for the rest of the region. But by the start of the Arab uprisings, rhetoric had supplanted any serious reform process. The status quo forces resisted any serious change in the way the country had been run, and reform plans—despite, or perhaps because of, their holistic and inclusive attributes and measurable benchmarks—were shelved.

When Jordan introduced the concept of a National Agenda in 2005, it was a novel approach to address political, economic, and social reform. This was also a "reform from above" effort; it included several elements that promised a smooth and gradual transition to real reform. The king appointed a national committee, which I headed, that comprised people from across the political, social, and economic spectrum (including individuals from government, parliament, media, political parties, and the private sector, as well as women activists) to develop the reform framework.[11] It was the first effort by an Arab country to initiate such an inclusive, holistic, and measurable reform process. The committee's final report did not limit itself to general statements but presented a comprehensive framework, complete with specific initiatives that were included in the national budget, performance indicators, and time frames for reform.

While Jordan was ahead of the curve in presenting both a vision and a road map for how reform from above could be successfully initiated, it conspicuously failed to muster the political will needed to implement such a vision and overcome the predictable obstacles. The beneficiaries of the status quo resisted moving the country away from a rentier system, which offered privileges in exchange for blind loyalty, and toward a merit-based system that would have threatened those privileges. When the National Agenda suggested a new election law that would gradually strengthen parliament by allocating some seats to national lists rather than just to district

candidates, the traditional political elite—the "rentier layer"—
managed to shoot down not just the electoral changes but the
whole National Agenda effort.[12]

Seven years later, as I write this book two years into the
Arab uprisings, Jordan still seems stuck in a system that has
promised far more reforms than it has delivered. Despite his
wide legitimacy and popularity, the king has not yet been able
to sustain a reform process that would bring a gradual transition to democracy without the shocks that countries like Egypt
and Tunisia have faced. The intelligence services continue to
play a role far beyond their security mandate, interfering in all
political matters and decisions large and small. Jordan's hesi-
tant approach, compared to Morocco's, has left the public increasingly frustrated. Social tensions and an increasing loss of
respect for the state have manifested themselves through such
incidents as attacks against government buildings and property, and tribal fights inside university campuses.

Jordan has not seen large-scale demonstrations since the
Arab uprisings began. But there are constant small ones. The
occasions for protest have ranged from calls for a redistribu-
tion of power among the three branches of government to demands for social equity, more attention for rural areas outside
the capital, and combating corruption. Protests have focused
on changes within the regime rather than on regime change.[13]
Since January 2011, in response to these protests, the government has implemented a few reforms, some of them meaningful though hardly sufficient. The constitution was amended by
a committee appointed by the king—this time without any opposition party members. Still, the amendments did establish
a constitutional court—long a demand of political activists—
and an independent commission to supervise all aspects of the
election process. But they omitted several necessary measures.

While the king lost the ability to postpone elections indefinitely, his other powers have been left intact. For example, the monarch still appoints and dismisses the prime minister and all members of the upper house of parliament. While the king has talked about a parliamentary government in the future, it is still to be seen how this will be implemented, given that the electoral law will not lead to a political-party-based parliament for several years. Also, while the amendments slightly limited the role of the security services in political affairs, they have hardly been curbed.[14] These services have in the past directly interfered by rigging elections, "instructing" some members of parliament on how to vote, vetoing government appointments, and acting as the arbiters on many government political decisions.

On the key issue of the election law, not much has changed. Though the king established a National Dialogue Committee in March 2011 to reach consensus on a new election law, a recommendation to enact proportional representation was shelved almost as fast as the recommendations of the National Agenda.[15] Instead, three successive governments have since tried their hand at a new law before finally passing one that only slightly deviates from the old one. Eighty-two percent of parliament would be elected exactly according to the old, unpopular formula, with 18 percent of the seats allocated to national lists. The new law, which was put forward with little consultation, angered secular groups, traditional proregime groups, and Islamist forces alike. Elections that were held in January 2013, though conducted in an atmosphere far freer than earlier ones, produced a parliament that was not much different than the one it replaced. A poll taken by the Center for Strategic Studies in Jordan showed that only 28 percent believed the current parliament would be better than the last one.[16] Without an election law that would pave the way for stronger parliaments, political reform appears stuck, and promises for a stronger, more representative parliament ring hollow.

Only two alternatives are open to the public in Jordan. The state has not relinquished the monopoly on political and economic power that it has enjoyed for decades, largely by offering jobs, health and education benefits, and social status in exchange for loyalty, coupled with the unchecked use of intelligence services to regulate public life. The regime appears unable to confront the unsustainability of the rentier system and has not grasped that power sharing is necessary for the stability and prosperity of the country. The religious opposition, strengthened for decades by its exclusion from the system, thus allowing it to claim martyrdom and to promise to purify politics without ever having to try, also lacks solid political and economic programs.

The state continues to resort to scare tactics, saying Islamists are congenitally opposed to democratic norms. Islamists, on the other hand, are increasingly emboldened by the Arab uprisings and are demanding a share of the political pie rather than their accustomed cosmetic participation in parliament. Rhayyel Gharaibeh, one of the current leading Jordanian Islamists, told me that the Brotherhood in Jordan is "totally committed" to political, cultural, and religious diversity, although many secular elements doubt that this commitment is categorical.[17] He claimed that the state exercises the same undemocratic practices it accuses his group of contemplating.

Given that political party life was suspended for decades in Jordan (from 1957 to 1989), leaving only Islamists any opportunity for organized political activity, the prospects for breaking the state–Muslim Brotherhood duopoly appear extremely dim. If activists are creating third party forces in Egypt or Morocco, they have yet to be heard of in Jordan. True, the country has witnessed the emergence of youth groups, frustrated and unwilling to settle for the life their parents lived. But they are terribly disorganized, defined more by their frustration and anger toward the system than by any clear vision for the country's future. They appear in no hurry to organize into formal political structures, yet they grow increasingly frustrated with a system they no longer feel is attentive to their needs.

To be sure, the king has to balance the demands of political activists who want a larger say in their country's governance with those of conservative groups who see no contradiction in wanting corruption addressed without endangering their privileges under the rentier system. This is not an easy task, and the king cannot do it alone. But he has chosen to deal with this challenge largely by appeasing the conservatives, retaining almost no one within his inner circle who solidly believes in political reform. The king has often declared his intention to implement gradual and serious reforms. So far, this has not systematically taken place.

Moreover, the government has no clear plan for dealing with the country's economic problems. High unemployment and a gaping budget deficit have remained largely untouched. The country cannot continue to channel large numbers of university graduates into guaranteed government jobs and maintain expansionary, often unproductive fiscal policies. The budget deficit has risen from about 3.5 percent of GDP at the time Jordan graduated from the IMF program in 2004 to about 11.5 percent at the end of 2012. Public debt has gone from $10 billion in 2004 to more than double that amount in 2012. A move away from a rentier, privilege-based system to a merit-based one is not simply an economic decision. It will take great political will for Jordan to wean itself from its traditional reliance on outside aid from Gulf states and the West to finance largely unproductive expenditures, and move toward a self-reliant economy. Today, largely as a result of the uprisings, it is clear that such political and economic policies have become unsustainable.

If reform from above had any real chance of succeeding, it would be in a place like Jordan. Though the country does not have a strong parliamentary tradition, the Hashemites (the royal ruling family in Jordan and descendants of the prophet Muhammad) have always advocated liberal social policies, including for Christians and women. While the system did not allow much political competition, it did not engage in abusive practices against its opponents and does not have a culture of imprisoning and brutalizing political prisoners. Because the Muslim Brotherhood was historically allowed to operate legally in the country—albeit as a charity organization—the Islamists adopted moderate policies in comparison to their sister organizations in other Arab countries, and for a long time saw themselves as part of the regime.

In short, the country has all the elements to be a model for political and religious tolerance, but it has refrained from taking sustained steps on the political front. Yet the Jordanian ruling system cannot continue unchanged. The population is better educated than most neighboring populations, and its citizens are aware of their rights and are demanding a larger say in their affairs. Cosmetic reform will no longer work. Many in the regime still surprisingly act as if reform can be not just slow but glacial. Jordanian officials have so far maintained that the protests that took place last year were limited to few hundred people and that discontent is largely restricted to a few outspoken elites. Such a blind spot shows them to be seriously out of touch with the country. If reform from above is to succeed in Jordan, it will require a dramatic shift of priorities by a system that has so far resisted change—a shift that can be led only by the king.

Emerging Trends

No two countries in the Arab world have undergone identical transition processes. Some regimes, such as those of Egypt, Tunisia, Yemen, Syria, Libya, and Bahrain, claim they were taken by surprise, while others, like Morocco and Jordan, claim they have stayed ahead of the protests. Regardless, it is clear that no country is immune to change. The path ahead for each will depend largely on how quickly and wisely it reacts.

With the possible exception of Morocco, which moved quickly to institute some reforms, the recurring theme in most countries is the assumption that somehow they are immune to the changes affecting their neighbors. Gulf states such as Saudi Arabia and Bahrain still gamble that with sufficient financial resources, strictly limited residency requirements for migrant workers, and draconian security measures, they can not only weather the storm but even reverse the move toward change. Jordan seems more preoccupied with convincing others that it is serious about reform than with implementing it.

The learning curve has sometimes been too steep. Countries with time remaining are not using it to manage serious reform processes from above, while countries that have undergone transitions are still struggling to steer toward calm waters. Those that have chosen approaches that are more holistic and inclusive, as well as logically sequenced, such as Tunisia, seem to be doing better than those where such processes at times defied logic, such as Egypt. The turmoil of the transitions should not, however, eclipse the Arab Awakening's many accomplishments.

Elections are now taking place in countries that have not witnessed them in decades—such as Libya—or are being conducted in a freer manner than ever before. The establishment of independent election commissions to supervise all aspects of the electoral process, rather than relying on interior ministries to do this, was unheard of two years ago and is quickly becoming common practice. Morocco, Libya, Tunisia, Egypt, and Jordan all set up such commissions to supervise elections. This is no insignificant development. Where presiding over a country for life was the standard practice among almost all leaders in republican states in the region, term limits are becoming the new norm. Political parties, formerly regarded as an irritant at best, are now seen as a necessity to advance political life.

While many Arab nations have moved away from the secular despotism that has characterized the region for decades, we have yet to see whether they are moving closer to political, cultural, and religious pluralism and inclusive economic prosperity, or toward other forms of despotism. This second awakening of the Arab world displays many trends that should occasion optimism; yet the region's embryonic forces for pluralistic democracy face enormous political and economic obstacles.

II

From Awakening to Pluralism

5
Education for Pluralism

In order to thrive, democracy must exist in "a culture that accepts diversity, respects different points of view, regards truths as relative rather than absolute, and tolerates —even encourages—dissent."[1] Without such a culture, it is impossible to build a system that redistributes power. The political transitions taking place in the region today—toward parliamentary and presidential elections, coalition governments, constitution writing, and the like—will not, by themselves, necessarily lead to sustainable pluralistic systems, even if such commitments to pluralism are spelled out in the new constitutions. What makes these commitments permanent is accepting different points of view and respecting the will of the people to choose their governments *and* to change those choices depending on the record of those governments in power.

Respect for diversity is not an innate characteristic. Humans have a well-developed sense of "us" and "them," dressing and speaking like members of their social/ethnic group, trusting and bonding with them. Appreciating differences is a taught behavior. It must be fostered by the community, particularly at school. But respect for diversity is glaringly lacking in Arab educational systems. Instead, youth in the Arab world learn that national and regional unity take precedence over differences in culture and opinion. Diversity in thinking is often viewed negatively. Most Arab educational systems actively promote simplistic analyses and eschew diversity of opinion and critical thinking.[2] The lack of intellectual building blocks of pluralistic, democratic societies implies that educational reform is a prerequisite for building such societies.

Improved educational systems would not, of course, bring instant political change. A recent study on education in Saudi Arabia and the Gulf concluded that the full impact of successful education reform might take half a century to emerge.[3] This is all the more reason to focus urgent attention on allocating the appropriate funds and human resources to the effort now. With proper reforms, education has the capacity to create generations of participating citizens and produce a workforce that is capable of developing and expanding national economies. The lack of political participation and a depressed economy were two main catalysts for the popular uprisings.

But there is a long way to go. The old political establishments and powerful religious institutions have preferred to protect their monopoly on "the truth" rather than create educational systems that would give students the freedom and intellectual tools to question past practices, effectively challenge authority, and innovate or add value in the private sector. As a result of these self-preservationist practices, the schools have prevented entire generations from achieving their potential. Students have not been equipped to improve institutional practices or compete in the domestic or global market. The basic aim of the school systems has been to educate students to be docile and not to question what they are told.

Religious establishments, often in tandem with Arab governments, have also tried to preserve their monopoly on interpreting religious thought and practice. They interpret religion narrowly, not allowing for different interpretations, in a manner not commensurate with the practices of early Islam or even with the main religious scholars of only one hundred years ago. In the late 1800s, for example, Muhammad Abdu, the Egyptian Muslim scholar who became the head of Al-Azhar, highlighted Islam's natural compatibility with individual and communal critical thinking and reasoning.[4] Muhammad Rashid Rida, Abdu's disciple, argued that Islam allows people to interpret it to meet their changing needs with time, thereby endorsing the concept of *ijtihad* (rational rulings).[5] Ali Abd al-Razeq, an Egyptian Islamic reformer (1888–1966), defended the abolition of the caliphate by Turkey, asserting that there is no specific political system that can be labeled Islamic.[6] But the modern Islamic reform movement, which managed to restructure Al-Azhar's curriculum and establish a new modern college and a school of sharia law in Cairo, did not last long. Al-Azhar's conservatives persecuted the scholars who had a critical approach to tradition.[7] And the emergence of the Muslim Brotherhood, which was established in 1928, marked the end of the reformist movement.[8] The Brotherhood aimed to build an Islamic society in Egypt prior to establishing a caliphate in all Muslim-majority countries.[9]

Yet if the objective of Arab governments and the contemporary religious establishments was to create and maintain docile societies, the recent uprisings irrefutably demonstrate that Arab publics are no longer willing to remain silent about the inability of their political systems to provide both freedom and bread. Weak educational systems have directly led to Arab governments' failure to provide jobs.[10] Unemployment figures

for young people between the ages of fifteen and twenty-four
in the Arab world stand at more than 25 percent, double the
world's average—this in a region where 70 percent of the population is under thirty years of age.[11]

Not only were the original policies ignoble in their goals,
they also failed at their primary aim of creating a docile population. Antiquated ideas about achieving growth while con-
trolling the population through outdated education systems
must be discarded. If Arab governments truly want to create
new political and economic foundations for pluralistic and
prosperous Arab societies, the whole approach to education
must be revisited.

In Iraq under Saddam Hussein, for example, one of curriculum objectives for kindergarten was to "instill love of the
president leader Saddam Hussein in the child's mind."[12] In
Egypt under Mubarak, eleventh-grade students learned about
the achievements of their president in the course on national
education. The course textbook stated that "the Mubarak era
has witnessed a lot of gigantic achievements in the economic,
investment and service sectors. The impact of these achievements was felt by citizens throughout Egypt."[13]

New allocations for education need to be properly channeled toward improving not only education quantitatively—
building schools, closing the gender gap, and eradicating
illiteracy—but also the quality of education—teaching skills
such as critical thinking, rigorous research, and the ability to
communicate. Formal education must also instill respect for
diversity and acceptance of different points of view.

These skills and values are prerequisites to building a
better Arab world. Arab governments need to internalize the
idea that promoting their populations' ability to question and
to seek knowledge is the only way to ensure prosperity, even if

it might strengthen criticisms of the governments themselves. The alternative is a stagnant society that falls further behind, both economically and politically. In the end, Arab governments have no choice but to accept that the headache of a critical populace that may turn them out of power at the ballot box is preferable to the cancer of an ignorant, impoverished, angry populace that may turn them out of power through violent rebellion. The uprisings proved this point beyond any doubt.

Short-Lived Education Reform

The Arab Awakening that George Antonius wrote about began as a revolution in education. Various Arab thinkers in the Levant in the nineteenth and early twentieth centuries advocated for a universal education system that promoted free inquiry and active social participation. Abd al-Rahman al-Kawakibi (1849–1902), for example, was a Syrian intellectual and pan-Arabist who emphasized education as the main solution to tyrannical rule and the antidote to what he viewed as a stifling social structure. He envisioned universally available education that would bolster critical thinking and inquiry. His reform ideas were not based on merely transplanting European knowledge into the Arab world; rather, he called for distinctly Arab curricula that embraced the region's unique history, culture, and language.[14]

During the nineteenth century, waves of Christian missionaries from Europe and America established new schools and colleges in Lebanon, Syria, and Palestine. American missionaries created the Syrian Protestant College in 1866 (this later became the American University of Beirut), while the French founded Saint Joseph University in Beirut in 1875.

These institutions became major universities with significant influence over higher education systems as well as the political and social features of the Arab Levant. Each graduated generations of Arab political leaders. Both introduced liberal arts curricula that encouraged critical thinking and scientific reasoning.

In Egypt, Muhammad Ali, the Khedive of Egypt in the first half of the 1800s, embarked on a comprehensive modernization project that included education. Influenced by the French, he founded primary and secondary schools as well as specialized institutes of higher education such as the school of medicine and that of administration and linguistics. Until the mid-twentieth century, Egypt remained at the forefront of education reform, influenced first by the French and then by the British.

Cairo was a major center for art, literature, and the publication of books, journals, and newspapers. Noted political and religious reformers such as Muhammad Abdu, Rifa'a Tahtawi, Ali Abd al-Razeq, Taha Hussein, and Lutfi al-Sayed made significant contributions to political, religious, and education reform. The reforms these scholars suggested or implemented encompassed both structural and contextual developments. Taha Hussein, for example, conceived of an educational system in which regional exchanges in books, curricula, students, and teachers would abound. He advocated education that promoted foreign language learning while maintaining an emphasis on Arabic as the native tongue of Egyptian youth. In addition to such technical reforms, he supported elements within the curriculum that would prepare students for democratic governance and promote civic participation, even if it disturbed the status quo.[15]

These education reform efforts did not survive long into

the twentieth century. The political monopoly that Arab governments exercised after independence was coupled with an education strategy that focused on quantity rather than quality. They abandoned the ideas of previous generations of Arab educational thinkers and failed to develop vibrant and comprehensive educational systems. Sadly, after independence, Arab countries' educational systems mirrored their authoritarian, monolithic political systems. In Bahrain, among many other countries, one finds an exaggerated glorification of the country's leaders. For example, children in fourth grade have to identify the king, crown prince, and prime minster ("May God save them") from their pictures; memorize the biography and achievements of the king; and know their duties toward him.[16]

The Current Educational Systems

While educational systems differ from country to country, there are some general shared characteristics regardless of their levels of political, economic, and human development or particular historical trajectories. These characteristics undermine creativity, suppress free thinking, and produce poorly trained graduates. This failure cannot be blamed on an unwillingness to allocate sufficient funds, however, as Arab states have actually invested heavily in education—about 5 percent of GDP over the past forty years. In comparison, the rich countries belonging to the Organization for Economic Cooperation and Development (OECD) devote about 6 percent of their collective GDP on education, which includes both public and private funds.[17]

Arab countries' spending has achieved impressive gains in access to free primary education and, to a lesser extent, secondary education. The adjusted net enrollment rate in primary schools in Arab states reached 86 percent in 2009, up 9 percent from 1999.[18] In secondary schools, the gross enrollment rate jumped from 22 percent in 1970 to 68 percent in 2009, when almost thirty million students attended secondary school.[19] Tertiary enrollment multiplied seventeenfold between 1970 and 2009, with women being the greatest beneficiaries.[20]

Despite this progress, Arab states still have the world's second-lowest preprimary participation rate and primary school enrollment rate, after Sub-Saharan Africa.[21] Gender equality has also not been realized in many states, and the overall adult illiteracy rate in the Arab region remains high— 27 percent in 2009.[22]

Even in areas that have been the focus of reform efforts —mathematics and sciences, for example—the results have been disappointing. Fourth- and eighth-grade students from the Arab states who participated in a survey called the Trends in International Mathematics and Science Study (TIMSS) in 2003, 2007, and 2011 scored significantly below the international average.[23] Fourth-graders who participated in the OECD-coordinated Program for International Student Assessment (PISA) in reading, mathematics, and science in 2003 and 2009 also scored considerably below the global average.[24] The same outcome was seen in fifteen-year-olds from Arab states who participated in the testing program Progress in International Reading Literacy Study (PIRLS) in 2006 and the fourth-graders who took that test in 2011.[25]

Even given the variations among states, these results irrefutably show that the achievements produced by Arab educational systems are generally low.[26] The best fourth-graders in all Arab states that participated in TIMSS 2007 fell below even the average proficiency level of fourth-grade students from the top five performing countries in both mathematics and the sciences.[27]

It seems clear that whether we are referring to such humanities or social sciences as literature, civic education, and history, or technical subjects such as mathematics and sciences, the Arab states' educational systems have failed to produce graduates that would be competitive in the job market. It is worth examining those specific characteristics that do the most to suppress rigorous independent thinking, tolerance, teamwork, and respect for different points of views.

ROTE LEARNING

When I was growing up in Jordan, memorization was the most important skill necessary to acquire good grades. We were repeatedly asked to recite pages from texts, almost verbatim. Use of other texts was seldom encouraged or suggested. Teachers emphasized rote learning and neglected the development of more flexible skills such as problem solving.[28] Findings by the World Bank indicate that my experience was shared across the Arab world. The World Bank notes that the main activities in the classrooms in MENA (Middle East and North Africa) continue to be copying from the blackboard, writing, and listening to the teachers. Group work, creative thinking, and proactive learning are rare. Frontal teaching—with a teacher addressing the whole class—is still a dominant feature, even in countries that have introduced child-centered pedagogy.[29]

There are plenty of examples in the Arab world of such methods, which produce graduates who not only are unaccustomed to questioning whatever "truth" is given to them but are often penalized if they do. A study in Egypt concluded that students spend most of their time memorizing and reciting texts with little regard to any other skills.[30] Another study documents how Syrian students are encouraged to regurgitate precisely the same language that is used in their textbooks, and even a correct answer is considered wrong if words are added or removed.[31]

ABSENCE OF INDEPENDENT THINKING

Educational systems in the Arab world tend to be authoritarian. The teacher's word is supreme, and there is little room for dialogue, discussion, or dissent. The contents of textbooks are presented as indisputable fact.[32] The same study on Syria showed that most high school classes are teacher-directed lectures with limited student engagement. Questions are allowed in class, but students may not say to their teachers, "I do not agree with you."[33] It is a system that produces men and women unlikely to threaten established practices.

Another study found that the Saudi Arabian curriculum is designed to preach unity of thinking, to "confuse opinion with fact, and to see ethical questions in black and white," promoting an understanding of Islam as a "stagnant body of knowledge."[34] According to the curriculum, philosophy and logic lead to social schisms and should be avoided. The overall lesson is that intellectual debate must be sacrificed for the sake of national unity.[35]

OBEDIENCE TO THE REGIME

Most Arab states' curricula instill obedience to the regime and do not use education to develop responsible, informed, and civic-minded citizens.[36] The outgoing regimes in Tunisia, Egypt, and Libya consciously created systems that produced dependent and submissive students ill suited to challenge their authority.[37] This has hardly changed with the arrival of new leaders.

Participatory activity available to students in Tunisian public schools was limited to cultural associations and sports clubs. Students were not allowed to engage in debates, nor were their opinions respected if they differed from those of their teachers.[38]

In Egypt, teachers, curricula, and activities in public schools failed to promote democratic values and practices.[39] A serious gap exists between the concept of citizenship education espoused by Egypt's Ministry of Education and the actual content of the country's social studies textbooks. School texts published in 2006–7 emphasized tourist attractions rather than citizenship concepts, on the premise that tourism is a major source of national income.[40] The books rarely mention such basic aspects of citizenship education as rule of law, social justice, or political participation. At the same time, citizens' dependence on the government for the provision of goods and services was exaggerated. The term *Al-Sultah* (authority) appears twice as often in social studies textbooks as the term *Al-Muwatin* (citizen)—a clear indicator of state dominance over citizens.[41]

In Libya, Muammar Qadhafi destroyed many modern features of the education system. He ordered the burning of major reference works in science, stopped teaching the English language in schools, and ended civic education. All school subjects had to include some material from his Green Book, a short document published in 1975 to outline his political philosophy, including essays in the Arabic language textbooks used for reading comprehension, while his own statements about science were inserted into science textbooks.[42]

Social studies and national education textbooks in Bahrain, Oman, and the United Arab Emirates emphasize national, cultural, and Islamic identity. The textbooks do not, however, highlight citizen rights or democratic values such as freedom of expression and tolerance of other points of view. They present civic issues in a theoretical and superficial manner, with no accompanying hands-on activities. There is no clear explanation of decision making in the state or how students can participate in the political process. Teachers receive no training in citizenship education or on teaching citizenship skills in their classrooms.[43]

In Morocco, when a teacher once asked students in a civic education class to express their opinions, the surprised students responded that it was the first time anyone requested their personal views or encouraged them to speak up.[44] In Jordan, the civic and national education textbook for the tenth grade emphasizes that "citizenship has two aspects: one is allegiance and the other is belonging [to the nation]."[45] This definition blatantly ignores the rights dimension of citizenship.

RELIGIOUS EDUCATION

Most Arab states offer religious education in their K–12 schools. In countries with a diversity of religions, such as Lebanon and Egypt, Christian students are taught about Christianity while Muslims are taught about Islam. In countries where non-Muslims are not nationals or constitute a small minority, such as Tunisia, Morocco, Libya, and the Gulf countries, only Islamic education is offered. In learning about their own religion, however, students are not taught to accept and respect other religions, and references to other religions tend to be subjective, inaccurate, and sometimes derogatory. According to the Egyptian textbooks on Islamic education, there is only one true religion—Islam, which God revealed to Adam and all the prophets including Moses, Jesus, and Muhammad. One eighth-grade textbook quotes a chapter of the Qur'an, explaining, "And whoever desires other than Islam as religion—never will it be accepted from him, and he, in the Hereafter, will be among the losers."[46]

Religious education in Egyptian public schools for grades 1–12 encompasses three major topics: beliefs, rituals, and code of behavior in society. In a country where 10 percent of the population is Christian, Muslim students are taught about Christianity only through the perspective of the Qur'an and Hadith (the Prophet Muhammad's sayings). In their own religion courses, Christian students do not learn about Islam at all, as it postdates their religious texts. The situation is similar in Lebanon. Public school students in both countries receive little introduction to religions other than their own.[47]

In Egypt, however, students of all faiths receive a good deal of knowledge about Islam from their Arabic language and social studies textbooks. Many of the Arabic lessons in primary schools use verses from the Qur'an and the Hadith to teach social values such as charity and honesty, but there are also verses that contradict the Christian belief in the Holy Trinity. History courses focus on Islamic civilization since the advent of Islam, while the history of Copts is limited to its economic and social aspects. This educational approach to the Christian minority does not take into account the religious identity of Muslims and Christians as reflected in their religious beliefs and lifestyles.[48]

In Saudi Arabia and many of its neighboring countries, one of the main objectives of education policies is to safeguard the society's Islamic identity. This necessitates an elaborate curriculum in Islamic education that emphasizes the particular Islamic vision and practices of the ruling family. For example, the fundamentalist Wahhabi perspective is emphasized in Saudi Arabia while references to other Muslim sects, such as Shiism, are very critical. This is in a country with a significant Shiite minority.

In Syria, Islamic education explicitly bolsters President Bashar al-Assad's political power—Islamic textbooks produced by the Syrian Ministry of Education are filled with lessons about obeying the Baath leadership.[49] Students even learn that an obedient Muslim must follow the Muslim ruler, even to the point of fighting Muslims who would rebel against him.[50]

There have been some steps in the right direction. A recent initiative by the Egyptian Family House, a national group comprising Al-Azhar, churches from different Christian denominations, and a number of academics, calls for a new religious education program that focuses on values common to Muslims and Christians. A committee was formed to design the program and have it approved by the government for implementation in schools in the fall of 2012. It has not been implemented so far. Unfortunately, such efforts remain the exception rather than the norm.

What Is Missing?

The challenge of improving education in the Arab world is compounded because officials do not always focus on where reform is most needed. Most of the initiatives that Arab governments label "education reform" address mainly technical aspects of education. After recognizing the poor academic performance of their secondary school graduates in mathematics and sciences, as well as the global demand for communication and information technology skills, a number of Arab countries embarked on reforms aimed at improving students' outcomes in mathematics, sciences, English language, and information and communications technology.[51] Education reformers developed new curricula and equipped schools with computers, laboratories, and other cutting-edge technology. The wealthy Arabian Peninsula countries as well as private schools throughout the region promoted the use of technology in the classroom. Several countries introduced English as a basic subject matter in public primary schools.

A 2008 World Bank study reported that the Middle East and North Africa region, which includes eighteen Arab countries, introduced thirty-four education reform programs in fourteen countries with more than nine hundred reform measures, an average of sixty-five per country.[52] Reform programs covered topics such as pedagogy, teaching capacity, and management.[53] There were some impressive achievements in closing the gender gap and halving illiteracy rates.[54] But for all the money spent, students' average learning outcomes did not improve.

For example, several education reform initiatives in Jordan and Palestine have aimed to build capacity, reduce illiteracy, expand early childhood care and basic education, and eliminate the gender gap. But civic and national education textbooks are still full of theoretical information for students to memorize. The books underscore citizens' duties—loyalty to the nation and respect for state laws—with little emphasis on activities that foster citizenship skills and promote democratic values and attitudes.[55] The situation is similar in Lebanon, where a big gap exists between curriculum goals and actual practice in the classroom.[56]

These findings, along with the World Bank assessment,

suggest that reform efforts by Arab governments are not improving the quality of education. The overwhelming share of reform measures in the prekindergarten, basic, and secondary grades focused on material improvements—construction of schools, provision of teaching materials, and so on. Reform programs fell short in addressing the overall quality of education. There was little improvement in performance indicators, citizenship skills, methods of teaching and assessment, status and qualifications of teachers, governance, or accountability.[57]

Moving Forward

As stated earlier in the chapter, the real problem for education reform is not a lack of financial resources; rather, it is a lack of political will to effect the deep changes necessary to promote diversity and dissent. Monetary investments have not produced the desired outcomes because the overall philosophy of the education systems still runs counter to them. The old guard and Islamist movements alike still see education's basic purpose as indoctrination rather than training people to think.

This means that physical improvements to the schools and even curriculum revisions are of limited value unless they are coupled with the national desire and political will to invest in the human infrastructure of a free, democratic citizenry. As Arab societies attempt to make up for lost time as a result of decades of political stagnation, they cannot afford to ignore their educational systems.

Arab intellectuals have long drawn attention to the poor quality of education in the Arab world and have suggested areas for improvement. One of the most important contributions in this field came from the 2003 Arab Human Development Report, written by Arab intellectuals and sponsored by the Arab Bureau of the United Nations Development Program. The report identifies three deficits in the region: freedom, knowledge, and the gender gap. In terms of "building a knowledge society" there are five pillars that should structure the edifice: freedom of speech, opinion, and assembly; high-quality education provided to learners at all levels and promoting life-long learning; a commitment to developing scientific research and keeping up with the information age; a shift toward production in the knowledge-based industry; and the establishment of an authentic and enlightened Arab general educational model.[58] The report offered little detail on how to achieve these goals, but the message is clear. Educational reform efforts cannot ignore these pillars if they are to create prosperous societies in the region.

Education without innovation and creation does not bolster economic productivity in today's world, and it would also hinder the emergence of prosperous societies. Teaching creativity can be as simple as assigning students the task of producing something—anything from artwork to videos. Problem solving and critical-thinking skills enable the learner to consider alternative ideas, think of unconventional solutions to unconventional problems, and articulate these solutions.[59] Problem-solving skills can be nurtured in analytical reasoning activities, math problems, and science. So in a sense, education reform must be deliberate and holistic. It has the potential to improve economic outcomes as well as the social and political culture of the Arab world.

Furthermore, schools should no longer restrict their mandate to the acquisition of facts. They should foster a definition of knowledge that includes social and emotional development as well. A growing body of research has shown that a positive school climate promotes academic achievement in reading, mathematics, and the sciences,[60] as well as in citizenship skills,[61] and it also reduces the frequency and intensity of school violence.[62] School climate—the character and quality of school life that reflect values, goals, organizational structure, interpersonal relationships, and teaching and learning practices[63]—is pivotal to either promoting or hindering education reform.

Arab countries would do well to learn from this growing body of literature. Teaching young students what it means to be citizens who participate in and contribute to their societies, rather than subjects of the state who are taught what to think and how to behave, is key to democratic progress. Young people first learn how to be productive members of a community in their school settings. That knowledge can then be replicated in the broader society. In these areas, however, education reform in the Arab world is glaringly lacking.

The process of democratization set in motion by the second Arab Awakening needs to take place at this deep level. The sustained intellectual, political, and economic development the Arab world needs for true modernization will require changes not only to the political structure—electoral law, constitutions, leaders—but also to the countries' educational systems. Education reform efforts must shift from technical changes to substantive ones that promote values and skills that are compatible with both the regional shift from autocratic to democratic ruling structures as well as the global shift from production to knowledge-based economies. These attributes are essential if the region is to move away from its traditional reliance on "rents," in the form of oil and outside assistance, and toward a system that empowers its citizens with the requisite skills to build self-generating, prosperous economies.

Any current and future education reforms in the Arab

world must face rigorous evaluation. Are students taught what it means to be a citizen? Do they learn at an early age—not just from formal teaching but, more important, through practice—that there is usually more than one side to any particular issue and that all sides should be explored and debated? Are they taught to question, inquire, participate, work in teams, and communicate? Are they taught to uphold freedom, equality, and respect for human rights? Or is "knowledge" spoon-fed to them in a manner that discourages questioning? Is the success of education systems measured only by the number of students enrolled, or also by the quality of the education they receive?

The Arab Awakenings demonstrate—beyond the shadow of a doubt—the failure of Arab governments' development policies. Education is at the top of these failures. The old education policies did not produce docile yet productive citizens but rather frustrated and underemployed ones. Without reform the hope of the second Arab Awakening will be lost.

A move away from the old way of thinking to a productive one necessarily entails equipping people at a very early age with the skills to be innovative, productive, and independent thinkers. Because the results of education reform will take decades, the sooner the Arab world begins, the better.

6

The Second Arab Awakening and the Arab-Israeli Conflict

Peace Now or Never

In December 2011, Hanan Ashrawi, Shlomo Ben Ami, Dan Kurtzer, and I sat around a table with about twenty other experts to discuss the direction of the Arab-Israeli peace process. The event was held by the Toledo International Centre for Peace in Madrid—twenty years after the city helped launch the Middle East peace process by hosting an international conference at which Palestinian, Syrian, Lebanese, Jordanian, and Israeli leaders were represented. The four of us had participated in that 1991 conference—Hanan as the Palestinian spokesperson, Shlomo as Israel's ambassador to Spain, Dan as part of U.S. Secretary of State James Baker's team (which organized the conference), and me as the Jordanian spokesman.[1] Our hotel was just across the street from the one that had housed the Jordanian and Palestinian delegations in 1991. The short space between the two buildings symbolized the distance not traveled in twenty years of peacemaking.

In the 2011 conference, peace experts from the usual countries joined us at the table to reflect on a process that had been designed—and in twenty years had failed—to resolve the Arab-Israeli conflict. Participants were short of fresh ideas. Most of our initiatives, tactics, devices, and arguments were tried and tired.

Peace was not supposed to be so difficult. In 1991 we were full of hope: finally a serious process was launched that would end the Israeli occupation of the West Bank, Gaza, Golan Heights, and Lebanese lands and establish a two-state solution that would allow both Palestinians and Israelis to live in peace and security. The international community talked about a lasting end to the conflict that would be implemented in five years. Many who found this timeline overly optimistic suggested that a ten-year framework was more feasible. No one imagined that twenty years later not only would we have yet to achieve peace, we would also be facing the harsh prospect that peace might not be possible at all.

Taking Stock

At the dawn of the Arab uprisings in early 2011, the peace process—such as it was—already faced daunting challenges. The Oslo agreements of 1993, developed between Palestinians and Israelis during secret negotiations that circumvented the Madrid process, were built on the notion that it is better to reach interim agreements on mutually agreeable details than to allow the conflict's core issues to stall all progress. Progress on these secondary measures was meant to build a level of trust that would allow negotiators to then tackle the big questions: the future of Jerusalem, borders, settlements, refugees, and security.

The Palestinians accepted this principle because the Palestine Liberation Organization finally gained recognition from the United States, Israel, and the international community as the representative of the Palestinian people. Five years were seen as an acceptable time to wait for independence and statehood. But events did not unfold this way.

While the on-again, off-again negotiations dragged on, the status quo on the ground did not remain frozen. Unilateral actions by Israel—particularly the ongoing expansion of settlements—meant the Palestinians watched the land whose future they were trying to negotiate disappear from their possession before their eyes. It was as if two people were discussing how to split a pizza while one of them was eating it.

Settlers in the West Bank and East Jerusalem have both grown in number and expanded in their geographical distribution. The number has increased from about 250,000 at the time of the Oslo Accords to more than 500,000 today. Settlers now constitute 25 percent of the West Bank's population, with almost 80,000 of them implanted in the heart of the territory, far from the Green Line, its border with Israel. This new reality impedes the two sides' ability to swap land in any potential agreement, since these pinpoints of land, now claimed by Israel, are too scattered to join up easily into contiguous territory. In addition, the approximately 200,000 Jewish settlers in East Jerusalem make up a full 43 percent of the area's population, further complicating any effort to apportion the city between Palestinians and Israelis.

As the population grew and became more widely dispersed, the settler movement also took more hard-line positions while increasing its influence on Israeli politics. In 2011, radical settlers started attacking Israeli government buildings in addition to Palestinian mosques and olive groves. Meanwhile, their political representatives and lobbying efforts have aimed to make it impossible for any Israeli government to agree to a political settlement that does not meet their requirements.

The Palestinians, and the Arab public in general, have lost hope in a process whose only result seems to have been to give Israel time to expand further into Palestinian lands. These actions have moved the parties away from a two-state solution. Any workable two-state solution must produce a viable Palestinian state that is not so riddled with settlements that it creates a security nightmare that threatens both sides' stability.

Not that the past twenty years have been a total waste. Through all the years of negotiations, the two sides have been able to define the parameters of a solution and have even come close to resolving most of the pending issues. Today, the average Palestinian and Israeli have a good idea of what a resolution would look like. And most Israelis and Palestinians in the occupied territories still believe in the need for a two-state solution. But they are not convinced it will ever materialize.

The mistrust between the two sides is greater than ever. Unilateral Israeli settlements, Israel's construction of a barrier wall, Hamas's refusal to recognize Israel, and suicide bombings by Palestinian hard-liners have convinced each side that it lacks a partner for peace. While the contours of a solution are visible, the path to the goal remains obscure.

The prospects for a two-state solution were dim even before the Arab uprisings. One of the primary challenges is the question of time. While time may have been on Israel's side, allowing it to alter the facts on the ground and position itself for a solution more favorable to its own interests, demographics now give the advantage to the Palestinians. Already the number of Arabs is about equal to the number of Jews living in areas under Israel's control.[2] Because of higher Arab birthrates, the Arab population is expected to outnumber the Jewish one in less than a decade.[3] Israel may be able to stifle the majority Arab population by perpetuating a two-tier citizenship model for another decade or two, but the end result is already obvious.

No minority group in history has been able to rule democratically over a majority population indefinitely. The Palestinians, unable to achieve their dream of an independent Palestinian state free of occupation, will demand the only alternative—equal rights and citizenship in the state of Israel. Such a "one-state solution" will mean the end of Israel as a Jewish state—anathema to most Israelis. To be sure, one can argue that Israel today is democratic only for its Jewish citizens. Its Arab population, while holding Israeli citizenship, is treated as a second-class minority, with truncated rights. But an ongoing two-tier citizenship model, which Israel might try to perpetuate in order to retain all the land, spells the end of Israel as a Jewish *and* a democratic state. An independent Palestinian state, an outcome Israel resisted for decades, has, ironically become the only guarantor of its Israeli identity.

The question I repeatedly asked Israeli officials and ex-officials during the 2011 Madrid meeting is this: What will Israel's long-term strategy be if a two-state solution becomes impossible? Does it even have a long-term strategy for its own survival? I never was given a clear answer to this question.

Several proposals have been put forward, none of them plausible. One is simply to forget about Gaza, leaving it to simmer in its own juices, and thereby eliminate more than one million Palestinians from the demographic formula. Many in Israel also propose unilateral disengagement from the West Bank, probably to the borders defined today by the Israeli separation wall, leaving all of Jerusalem and about 11 percent of the West Bank in Israeli hands. This approach would cause a humanitarian disaster and create a security nightmare right on Israel's doorstep. Israel's unilateral disengagements from southern Lebanon in 2000 and Gaza in 2005 brought it not peace but more security challenges, including wars in 2006 in Lebanon and 2008–9 in Gaza. This proposal would also leave all of Jerusalem, including Muslim and Christian holy sites, in Israel's hands, something neither the Palestinians nor any Arab or Muslim country would accept.

Another proposal is to create a two-tier citizenship system, under which Palestinians are given some civil but not political rights in Israel. Such a formula has never worked anywhere in the world. One needs only to point to South Africa under apartheid to see that no matter how strong a state is, no minority can dominate a disenfranchised majority forever.

A third proposal is to transfer some form of administrative control over Gaza and the West Bank to Egypt and Jordan. But both of those countries strongly oppose such a solution—to say nothing of the Palestinians' view. This move would be politically problematic with both countries' newly enfranchised publics.

A final, cruel scenario is a mass migration—either voluntary or forced—of Palestinians out of the West Bank or Gaza. None of these options offers a fair or realistic resolution to the conflict.

The Second Arab Awakening: One More Dimension

While the current threat to the two-state solution preceded the Arab uprisings, it is important to examine the uprisings' implications for the Arab-Israeli conflict. Have they helped or hurt the cause of a two-state solution? Is such a solution still possible? The answers depend largely on how Israel, the United States, and the international community react to these regional developments, and on the long-term strategies each adopts for dealing with them.

Many analysts point out that the Arab-Israeli conflict had little to do with the Arab uprisings. At the outset of the protests, few slogans were voiced about Israel, the United States, or the conflict. When anti-Israel sentiments were expressed at rallies, it was often in response to events such as the killing of an Egyptian policeman by Israeli security forces during a cross-border raid in September 2011, rather than voicing broader frustration with the conflict. Recent polls suggest that for many Arab citizens the issue has taken a backseat to employment and political reform.[4] But one should not think that the Arab world has stopped caring about the conflict, or that emerging regimes in the Arab world will be less critical of Israel.

Currently, Arab publics are naturally focused on their respective domestic challenges, such as a lack of political freedoms, poor governance, and economic hardships. But this does not mean they will somehow accept the Israeli occupation— or ignore it. As the storming of the Israeli embassy by angry Egyptians in September 2011 showed, Arab publics today are not quieter than those before the uprisings, and they are willing to challenge some of the basic notions of Israel's role in the region.

Elected regimes in countries undergoing transition will be more responsive to their publics, far less able to turn a blind eye to Israel's policies regarding the Palestinians and the region as a whole, and likely to resist addressing qualms through quiet diplomacy. The Israeli occupation—never accepted by the Arab world—cannot endure in an environment where people are calling for freedom and dignity. Inevitably, the growing contrast between the expanded political rights of Arab populations and the ongoing suffocation of Palestinians under occupation will make itself felt. The result will be a serious increase in hostile attitudes toward the occupation and the settlements.

Israel's reaction to these developments has thus far been largely defensive. In the past, Israel argued that it could not forge peace with dictatorships that do not represent their people. Thus a permanent peace could not be negotiated. Since the onset of the uprisings, however, the Israeli government has adopted the exact opposite argument: peace cannot be forged when countries are so unstable. One must wait, the claim is, until the dust settles.

While this argument appears logical at first glance, it smacks of the same time-buying strategy that underpinned the Oslo Accords' focus on technical details. It is also equally counterproductive. Israel's fear of a more hostile region will become a self-fulfilling prophecy if the emerging democracies see the Israeli government as implacably standing in the way of freedom for the Palestinians. There is also no reason to assume that the dust, left on its own, will settle on the side of peace. Proactive measures are needed to push it in that direction, particularly with conditions on the ground working against a peaceful solution.

Contrary to conventional wisdom, it is precisely when situations are in flux that they can be guided toward a specific outcome. If Israel is truly waiting for a better time for peace, rather than unwisely trying to run out the clock on a two-state solution, it may find that such a time will never come.

This is not to say that people are unaware of this consequence, or that all Israelis are oblivious to the potential disaster on the horizon. In America, *New York Times* columnist Thomas Friedman warned Israel it must "disentangle itself from the Arabs' story as much as possible" and forge a peace deal now for the sake of its own future. "There is a huge storm coming, Israel. Get out of the way."[5]

In June 2011, six months into the Arab Awakening, Tzipi Livni, then leader of the Israeli opposition in the Knesset, and I addressed a large audience at the Aspen Institute in Colorado about the urgency of new efforts for peace. Livni was very forceful in articulating why talks cannot be delayed.

> In the end, the choice for Israel is one of two options. One is for accepting, adopting, promoting, and implementing two nation-states in order to keep and preserve the wellness of Israel as a homeland of the Jewish people and a democracy. The other is not to make these decisions, which will lead to one state between the Jordan River and Mediterranean Sea. It's not going to be a Jewish State. It's going to be an Arab state.[6]

She also made the point to the American Jewish members of the audience—and beyond—that they are not doing Israel any favors by backing the Netanyahu government's hardline positions against peace, as time is not on Israel's side. If the conference organizers had hoped for a feisty debate, they were disappointed. I found it difficult to disagree with any of her arguments.

The fact is that the old Arab order is fundamentally changing, and while the new one is far from being fully formed, the changes are profound and permanent. Old policies cannot address new realities. The Arab world is discovering this—

mostly through turbulent transitions where political systems are finding it difficult to manage changes that began in the street. Israel, too, needs to understand that it must adopt different policies or else be increasingly seen as an outlier, occupying another people while less friendly democracies emerge around it.

Death of the Arab Peace Initiative?

In March 2002, Arab states attempted to break the deadlock in the peace process with a bold offer: the Arab Peace Initiative. The initiative promised Israel peace, nurmalization in relations, security with all Arab states (not only those that are territorially contiguous with Israel), a mutually agreed-upon solution to the refugee problem, and an end to the conflict and all territorial claims, in return for Israel's withdrawal from Arab lands it occupied in 1967 and the establishment of a Palestinian state alongside the Israeli one.[7]

The idea was simple but powerful. If the two sides cannot reach an agreement on their own, Arab states offered to provide the necessary regional security umbrella for both. This demonstrated to the Israeli public that the country could get a regional peace—rather than one with some of the Palestinians—in return for what they would perceive as painful compromises. It also provided the Palestinians with an Arab cover in return for their own painful compromises.

The Israeli government rejected the offer outright. Prime Minister Ariel Sharon cited the Arab Peace Initiative's reference to UN Resolution 194, which calls for the right of Palestinian refugees to return to their homes in Israel. He ignored the key phrase in the proposal stipulating that any solution to the refugee problem had to be mutually agreed upon. The Bush administration, for its part, paid lip service to the proposal and gave it lukewarm support. Israel did not present an idea of its own until two years later, when it executed a unilateral withdrawal from Gaza and built a wall—largely on Palestinian land—separating itself from the West Bank. For Sharon this was an attempt to eliminate more than a million Palestinians from Israel's demographic equation and thus extend the fuse on the time bomb.

Despite these negative responses, and an additional ten years of obstacles for the peace process, not one Arab country has withdrawn its signature from the Arab Peace Initiative. But patience hardly means that the initiative is a permanent offer.

The Arab Awakening is rapidly transforming the political context that produced the Arab Peace Initiative. Arab publics overthrew some of the leaders who signed on to it and are increasingly disparaging of an Israeli occupation that has become, like the status quo in the Arab world, unsustainable. While political and economic realities may dictate that the Egyptian-Israeli and Jordanian-Israeli peace treaties will continue to be honored (the Muslim Brotherhood–led government in Egypt has publicly committed to this, and it has not been a major question in Jordan), it will be nearly impossible to forge new treaties in the current climate. The initiative's main allure—an agreement with all Arab states—will become more unlikely as the perception of Israel erodes across the region.

The Role of the United States

The United States, caught off guard in January 2011, has been playing catch-up ever since. While the Obama administration acknowledges that it needs a change in strategy to achieve its objectives in the region—of stability, reform, and peace—such a plan has proven difficult to develop and implement. It is not easy to pursue a policy that prioritizes stability *through* reform rather than *over* it, and apply it across a region in which the United State has many conflicting interests. Moreover, the United States needs to acknowledge that the issue of peace cannot be compartmentalized and treated as if it had no links to reform or stability.

One administration official told me that the United States does not want to miss the opportunity to be on the right side of history as Arab publics fight for dignity and better governance. "We don't want to repeat the Iranian experience, where we toppled a popular leader in Musaddaq and stood by the Shah for the longest time and ended up alienating the Iranian people."[8] But that desire to act differently will be tested when it comes to peace in the Middle East. The United States cannot tell the Egyptians, Tunisians, Libyans, Syrians, Yemenis, and others that it supports their aspirations for freedom and dignity—but tell Palestinians that it is "complicated," that their universal human rights are constrained because of the identity of their oppressors. That is not a policy that will win the hearts and minds of the Arab world or help close the huge credibility gap the United States faces in the region.

In December 2000, when President Bill Clinton offered his own proposals, the parameters provided a useful framework for moving forward. While the parties failed to agree on a solution at that time, those parameters still offer a very good basis for a solution.

Six months into his presidency, Obama was forthcoming in a speech in Cairo, promising a new beginning in the region and a resolution of the Arab conflict. Then he settled into a desultory effort to get the parties back to a negotiating process that had exhausted its possibilities. While it was clear to most that the gap of trust between the two parties was too huge to bridge with still more negotiations, and that the creative intervention of a third party like the United States was crucial to a solution, no major American effort materialized.

The president's special envoy to the Middle East, the respected former senator George Mitchell, who earlier in his career successfully brought about a resolution to the Irish Protestant-Catholic conflict, wasted three years trying to revive a process that had lost all its credibility, rather than brainstorming an approach that reflected evolving dynamics. I met with Mitchell in April 2009, shortly after he was appointed, as he sought the views of those who had previously worked on the peace process. I told him that incrementalism would not work—the goalposts needed to be fundamentally shifted— and that the United States needed to pursue a regional solution using the Arab Peace Initiative as a frame of reference. He needed to clearly outline the expected endgame so that the process could regain some desperately needed credibility.

"You go for an incremental process, Senator, and Prime Minister Netanyahu will nickel and dime and give you nothing," I remember telling him. "If you want to listen to the traditional arguments about how to solve the conflict, you might as well go home, because this conflict will not be solved on the cheap, according to the traditional formulas." I then quoted Albert Einstein: "Insanity is doing the same thing over and over again and expecting different results." The key to the Arab states lies in Saudi Arabia, not Egypt, I told him, and urged him to forge close relations with the Saudi monarch. Mitchell affirmed that there was no going back to the incremental approach, that he understood there was not much time left, and that at some point the United States would have to put its ideas on the table. None of his subsequent actions reflected these understandings.

I met with him again a year later. By then, he was more resistant to the idea of putting forward a detailed and comprehensive package, although he did tell me that he made it clear to Netanyahu that the United States would not engage in a process with no end, and that he had two years in mind to solve the conflict. When I reminded him that twelve months had already passed, he still sounded confident that he could do it. He was very interested in my argument that under the Arab Peace Initiative, the offer of security guarantees by Arab states implies an obligation to transform Hamas and Hezbollah into political organizations that would not carry arms once a regional solution is achieved.

A year later, in May 2011, Mitchell resigned, without the United States having put forward any ideas. Dennis Ross, the president's special assistant who had been deeply engaged in the peace process since its inception, followed suit, resigning in November. Facing a barrage of important issues—the worst economic crisis since the Depression, an embattled health care initiative, and wars in Iraq and Afghanistan—as well as a hardline Israeli government and a weak Palestinian one, the White House apparently decided peace negotiations might take too much energy and that engaging deeply at that time was too politically risky. A coalition of some conservative Christian constituencies and hard-line supporters of Israel raised the potential electoral costs of applying necessary pressure on Israeli leaders. The Obama administration ended its first term with little to show for its efforts.

Still, nothing radical or novel is required. If today the United States were to present parameters in coordination with the other members of the so-called Quartet (the United Nations, European Union, and Russia), their content would not surprise anyone. They would have developed out of years of frustrating negotiations as well as such past initiatives as the Clinton Parameters or the Arab Peace Initiative. If coupled with a serious timeline and arbitration that provides a clear mechanism for holding the parties accountable for their commitments, such a proposal could provide the catalyst necessary for a solution that meets the needs of both the two parties and the constraint of time. The key obstacle remains Israel. The current Israeli governing coalition appears uninterested in accepting a historic settlement that would end its ideological insistence on keeping the entire land.

The One-State Solution?

More delay will soon render the two-state solution impossible. Many already believe it is too late. Some even argue that for the Israeli right, the current situation *is* the endgame, as any agreement on a viable Palestinian state will require compromises the right is not ideologically prepared to accept. As far back as 2003, Sharon demonstrated his reluctance to move beyond the status quo through his government's opposition to phase III of the road map, which would have resulted in a Palestinian state over most of the West Bank and Gaza. Statements by some of his closest advisers indicated Israel would not accept anything beyond a Palestinian state with "provisional" borders that constituted no more than half of the West Bank and that was shorn of East Jerusalem.[9]

If a two-state solution is no longer feasible, one alternative scenario that is gaining prominence among some Palestinian (and, interestingly, Israeli) leaders is the one-state solution. Palestinians and Israelis would be granted equal rights in a single state that encompasses Israel and all the occupied territories.

The first prominent Palestinian to demand that Palestinians be given equal rights in Israel was Sari Nusseibeh, now president of Al-Quds University in Jerusalem. When he first proposed the idea, in 1986, many Palestinians and other Arabs called him a traitor to Palestinian aspirations for independence. Today, more people see his point. About 25 percent of the Palestinian population in the Occupied Palestinian Territories agrees with a one-state solution for Israelis and Palestinians. It should be noted that 64 percent of Palestinians have no faith that an independent Palestinian state can be established in the next five years.

Polls suggest that a majority of Palestinians living in the West Bank and Gaza still want self-determination through an independent state of their own.[10] Most are not interested in the type of state the current Israeli government wants—one with limited sovereignty and no control of its airspace, and without Jerusalem, the Jordan Valley, and the possibility for refugees and displaced people to return to their original homes.

In this context, the idea of one state with equal rights for Israelis and Palestinians becomes more attractive. The possibility of such a solution is growing by the day—it is no longer a taboo subject. While the minority of Israeli politicians who have supported this idea also advocate a two-tier citizenship model where Palestinians can have civil but not full political rights, legally entrenched inequality is hardly sustainable in today's world.[11]

Time Is Not Infinite

Many analysts expected the Palestinian street, inspired by the Arab uprisings, to explode yet again. But a third intifada has not taken place, for reasons that are not entirely clear. Some attribute it to the Palestinians' fatigue with two very costly

intifadas that did not bring independence. The second intifada, which occurred in 2000, is widely seen by Palestinians as
having harmed their cause, particularly when various groups
resorted to suicide bombings that pushed the Israeli public
to the right and decreased international public support for
the Palestinian side. The erection of the wall and the rede-
ployment of Israeli troops from large Palestinian population
centers have also minimized contact between the two sides.
Adding to these potential explanations for the quiescence is
that the Palestinian economy, under the premiership of Prime
Minister Salam Fayyad, was doing relatively well until the
spring of 2012.

Were the Palestinians to start a peaceful intifada against
the occupation, much as the Egyptians and Tunisians did
against their regimes, it would be very difficult for Israel to
ignore. In addition, Israel would have a very difficult time
withstanding international pressure if a high number of Palestinian casualties were sustained over several weeks. It would
probably force the international community and the United
States to launch a fresh effort to solve the conflict.

Today, all sides seem incapable of moving forward. The
Palestinians' divided government, with Hamas ruling in Gaza
and the Palestinian Authority in the West Bank, is an additional factor—though not the main one—in the way of a lasting settlement. The Palestinian Authority seems to have given
up on whether Netanyahu would offer any settlement even
close to what the Palestinian public would accept. And the Israeli government has distracted itself and its constituents with
alarmism about the Iranian nuclear threat.

The second Obama administration may decide that this
issue is still too hot to handle. It might allow domestic political blackmail and the intransigence of the parties to dictate a

policy of continued caution. Though some of these constraints are formidable, particularly for a president confronted with the inevitable measure of strategic surprise that world events seem always to produce, the U.S. national interest is ill served by an ongoing policy of inaction. Time is not an infinite commodity, and it is dangerous to believe that one can go back to piecemeal peacemaking at any point in the future, ignoring a rapidly deteriorating situation on the ground.

Even granted all of America's domestic concerns, several considerations should trump the inclination to move slowly. Relations with the rapidly evolving Arab world have no chance of developing in a positive direction so long as the Arab-Israeli conflict is unresolved. The Arab world will be devastated if the United States should decide to conduct a military strike against Iran. While Israel will clearly remain a pivotal relationship for the United States in the region, the notion that the United States could afford hostile interactions with the newly enfranchised, vibrant Arab populations in the neighborhood is not tenable. Second, while the cause of moderation and of building pluralistic societies on the heels of the Arab Awakening will require a variety of developments, the persistence of the Arab-Israeli conflict will only encourage radicalism and put moderates on the defensive. Finally, it is difficult to reconcile the American Jewish community's concern about maintaining Israel's identity as a democratic Jewish state with its unwillingness to push the American government to foster a two-state solution before it is too late.

Tomorrow's Middle East will not be the same as yesterday's. Its ultimate shape is, of course, unknown. In the end, the 2011 uprisings against poor governance have created an opening to achieve not only democracy but also stability and peace. This crisis, like so many others, is a terrible thing to waste.

7

Third Forces and the Battle for Pluralism

How will history judge the uprisings that started in many parts of the Arab world in 2011? We now know that the label "Arab Spring" was too simplistic. Transformational processes defy black and white expectations. Do these movements resemble what happened in Europe in 1848, when several uprisings took place within a few weeks only to be followed by counterrevolutions and renewed authoritarian rule? Do they resemble the 1989 collapse of the Soviet Union, after which some countries swiftly democratized while others remained in the thrall of dictatorship? Whatever the case, it is clear that these processes will need decades to mature, and their success is by no means guaranteed.

The first Arab Awakening started with an intellectual renaissance that eventually found its way into popular movements, though they failed to bring democracy to the Arab world. The second Arab Awakening started with popular movements that have yet to find their way into intellectual frameworks. These movements are more unanimous about what they are against than about what they are for. But the debate to define this awakening has begun.

The principal fight in the Arab world is the battle for pluralism, not simply a fight against despotic rule. Decades ago, the region succeeded only in exchanging foreign despots for domestic ones. The second Arab Awakening must not emulate the first but go beyond it. It must anchor new policies with lasting respect for political, cultural, and religious pluralism, good governance, the rule of law, and inclusive economic growth. If any factor has contributed most to the years of stagnation in Arab society, it is the near-total absence of diversity and pluralism from political and cultural discourse. Truths are still regarded as absolute. A single person, party, or ideology is presented as the holder of all answers to all problems, while the public's role is largely to submit to those in power.

But the answer to the question of whether this battle for pluralism is indeed being waged after the revolts is tentative at best. Many forces claim to be committed to pluralistic principles—regimes that have not yet been toppled, political Islamists recently come to power, or third forces trying to carve a place for themselves—but this commitment has often proven to be little more than lip service. So far, the developments of the past two years suggest that when in power, most forces place their own interests ahead of democracy and pluralism.

The commitment to pluralism is a prerequisite for a sustainable political and economic renewal of the Middle East, and it must be demanded of everyone, Islamists and secularists alike. Instead of fearing Islamist participation and trying to marginalize various political groups, all countries need to ensure that no group can monopolize truth, rule indefinitely, deny the rights of others, or impose its cultural or religious views.

If there is real hope that societies will begin to respect, indeed embrace, diversity in the Arab world, the fight for democracy needs two simultaneous guarantees: everyone's right to peaceful political participation, and no one's right to monopolize truth or power. There must be an ironclad commitment to resist the temptation to use violence to shape the political environment. This includes security forces under government control, allied but plausibly deniable thugs, and flirtations with "uncontrollable" extremists.

Not enough is being done. Both the Islamist and the secularist sides are crystallizing in an increasingly polarized environment. Both need to work harder to advance democracy and accountability, rather than employing exclusionist words and behaviors that prevent the healthy development of societies. Neither "reform from above" nor "reform from below" is likely to succeed if these principles are not firmly adopted. If the new Arab order still insists on a winner-take-all approach and zero-sum outcomes, and if the principle of peaceful alternation of power does not become firmly entrenched, the second Arab Awakening will be for naught.

The Battle Is Not Against Islamists

As Islamists develop their economic and political programs, all other players must do the same. They must stop wasting their energies seeking ways to prevent an Islamist rise based on irrational fears of theocracy. It will do no good to pretend that Islamist parties do not enjoy broad popular support. Political Islam will not go away if Arab governments and the West ignore it. Repressing it through force will backfire. In a burgeoning democracy, Islamists have a right to be part of the process, and in any case they cannot be stopped from entering the political realm. Authoritarian regimes tried to exclude Islamists in the past, but the Arab public is clearly ready to move beyond the old exclusionary tactics.

Moreover, pushing Islamists out of the political process has historically resulted in cycles of violence and retaliation— a process that ultimately radicalizes the Islamists. The focus should instead be on bringing them in while cementing constitutional guarantees for pluralism and the right to organize that can be upheld at all times and for all people. The issue is not trusting Islamists' intentions but rather building a system that treats everyone the same and protects everyone's inviolable right to be included.

One should not fear Islamist parties in the Middle East simply because they are based in religion. Europe has many Christian Democratic parties that are socially conservative but advocate liberal social and economic policies—not much different from many Muslim Brotherhood parties. Currently, 18 of the 120 Israeli Knesset members belong to religious parties that typically possess hard-line views on the peace process— again not dissimilar from Islamist parties in the Arab world. In other words, it is not the presence of religious parties that matters but whether they are committed to democracy, the peaceful rotation of power, and the protection of individual rights.

This call for religious parties to be included is not an argument in support of their views. Selective democracy is no democracy at all. All political forces need to understand that if they accept the exclusion of others, they accept that they too may be excluded.

Third Forces

More than two years after the Arab uprisings, clear leaders of the battle for pluralism have yet to emerge. While secular forces claim to be the bearers of this torch, the continued hesitation by many of them to accept the participation of Islamists belies this commitment. All attempts to create a new Arab order—by old regimes trying to reinvent themselves, Islamist forces taking power after decades of semirepression, or third forces still struggling to develop clear programs and organizational capabilities—have stopped short of a categorical, unqualified, and genuine commitment to individual and minority rights and a rejection of force.

Operating in a region that lacks well-developed democratic practices, all political groups are suddenly forced to learn how to build their own constituencies while understanding that they cannot deny that right to others. To assume they will do so intuitively or immediately is wishful thinking. It is interesting to watch all forces in the Arab world today accusing others of exclusionist practices while employing the same type of exclusionist discourse. This was apparent in Egypt, where many secular forces acquiesced to the military's undemocratic practices because it served their short-term interests against the Islamists.

The change will have to play itself out, until political forces either suppress their opponents by coercion—and therefore achieve little from the second Arab Awakening—or realize that their own right to operate must include the same right for others, thereby resulting in pluralistic and stable societies.

It would be wrong to assume that these forces will take familiar forms or follow a predefined path. Moreover, the resulting institutions should not necessarily be modeled on Western structures and processes. While some universal values transcend culture, different regions in the world have been able to evolve into pluralistic societies without necessarily adopting all of the details of Western models. Democracy as developed in the Arab world must contain features that are unique to that region, or it is not likely to survive. Many formulas will be tried as Arab countries embark on their transitions. Western countries must not assume that Arab democracies will be identical to theirs, or that they must blossom instantly.

To have any hope of reshaping their societies—regardless of what unique details this ultimately includes—third forces in the Arab world must be founded on three basic values: pluralism, reliance on peaceful means only, and inclusion. These three values are embedded in the uprisings and can be found in the language of many of the protesters. Among the reasons cited for wanting to topple regimes was a desire for a functioning, honest government with limited powers that would grant every citizen the right to political participation. Many protesters chanted *silmiyyah* (Peaceful!) and carried flowers, sometimes in the face of deadly snipers, as in Syria for the first few months of the uprising. The movements that toppled the regimes were visibly inclusive, placing national identity above all other considerations (at least during the initial euphoria prior to bringing down the leader). These three values contributed significantly to the success of the uprisings.

PLURALISM

Pluralism can best be defined as the fundamental commitment to political diversity at all times. It means that no party has a monopoly on the truth and no party can impose its views on the rest of society. Such a commitment must include developing a system of checks and balances that redistributes power away from the executive and toward the legislative and judicial branches of government. Across the Arab world, the executive branch is too dominant, often with unelected and unaccountable institutions beholden to it. The intelligence services, for example, typically play a role in domestic affairs that far exceeds their security mandate. Any reform that does not end in true power sharing among the three branches of government cannot be deemed serious or successful.

To achieve a political space in which all are free to participate and none can monopolize the debate, these countries need protective constitutional mechanisms. They need a multiparty system, with majority rule but also one that protects or guarantees minority and personal rights; an independent judiciary; freedom of expression and of the press; the complete application of the rule of law; equality before the law and equal protection under the law for all citizens, regardless of gender, religion, ethnicity, or position; and serious respect for human rights. The protection of personal rights—such as freedom of worship, freedom of choice of clothing, right to privacy—is key. It would greatly allay the fears of not only the various Christian and Muslim groups but also secular Muslims who do not want their freedom of choice to be compromised by Islamist parties seeking to impose their religious views. But no matter which constitutional mechanisms a country adopts, they will not be respected unless there is also a balance among the political forces—for example, the ability of different political forces to coexist.

The third forces belonging to the old generation are not off to a good start. Many of them have favored their short-term interests over democracy, and many have shown themselves to be little different from the other dominant forces in Arab societies. That many are liberal will not be enough if they are not also democratic.

Thus the potential torchbearers of a pluralistic culture appear to be the new generation. This is the generation that started the uprisings, even if it has not yet shaped the course of the revolutions to address its needs and aspirations. When

I met in June 2012 with Ziad Ali, cofounder of the grassroots organization *Masrena* (Our Egypt), he seemed aware of the challenges. "We have to go through the learning process. It is not fair to judge this process harshly or quickly." But he also understood the priorities. "Our challenge is to build institutions quickly. The young are different from the old forces. We are coordinating very well. I assure you a critical mass is being built that believes in a better life for Egyptians, even if it is not in their lifetime. There is a paradigm shift in Egyptian society."

Ahmad Maher, another youth activist and a cofounder of the April 6 movement, mobilized young Egyptians through new technologies and social networking sites such as Facebook, YouTube, and Twitter. He too was clear on the path forward. "We need to build third parties," he told me. "We are seen so far as a spark, not an alternative. The youth and the liberals are weak, not organized, and fighting each other. Our main plan is to use the next five years organizing. We want to build a grassroots movement first, then a party."

Such talk seems to dominate the speech of the new generation, but it is hardly present among the older ones. The youth are likely to plant the seeds of pluralism. The Arab world will have to wait for decades, however, before the democratic experiment matures and societies enjoy a pluralistic culture with a manageable number of political parties.

PEACEFUL MEANS

Pluralism cannot survive unless all parties concede that only the state can carry arms, in line with Weber's "monopoly of the legitimate use of physical force" theory.[1] Actors such as Hamas, Hezbollah, and the various armed groups in Iraq must be fully disarmed and integrated into the political process in their own countries. Residual militias in Libya, Yemen, and Syria, despite winning popular support for opposing autocrats, must also disarm.

In May 2008, after the government ordered the shutdown of its telecommunications network, Hezbollah occupied West Beirut and effectively turned its weapons against the Lebanese people for several days. The Arab-brokered deal to end the fighting in Lebanon bolstered the group's political strength by granting Hezbollah veto power in the parliament. Nevertheless, the episode had negative consequences for the movement on the Lebanese street. Hezbollah lost some credibility in the eyes of the public and, by resorting to violence, set the democratic process back in Lebanon.

By the same token, governments must resist the temptation to use armed force to serve a partisan agenda. The police, intelligence services, and army must be inviolably neutral and must see their role as guaranteeing access for all to the political arena. Recourse to external proxies must be rigorously eschewed. When the governments of Libya and Syria used military power to suppress largely peaceful demonstrations, they forfeited their legitimacy as rulers and in effect authorized armed resistance. The new Libyan government, and any new Syrian one, will have a very hard time disarming the militias that have emerged as a result of their civil wars. The reconciliation process will also suffer.

Under a government committed to peaceful processes, no party can substitute guns for the ballot box or use force to repair an electoral defeat.

INCLUSION

The Arab world is a mosaic of ethnic and religious communities. These include Sunnis, Shiites, and other Muslim sects;

Christians of all denominations; Jews; and others. Ethnically, they include Amazigh (Berbers), Arabs, Armenians, Chechens, Circassians, Kurds, and many smaller groups. While the Arab world prides itself on its diversity, its politics and culture do not match the rhetoric.

Rights of minorities—and often majorities—have been systematically subordinated to the power of the ruling elites. How else can one explain the repression of the Kurds in Iraq and Syria, or the Amazigh in North Africa? How can one justify the treatment of Shiites as second-class citizens, often accused of serving as Iranian agents, in Saudi Arabia or Bahrain, or the Copts under successive Egyptian regimes? How can one explain the legal discrimination against women? Such official discrimination makes its sufferers feel they are less than citizens and prompts them to seek outside protection.

Societies prosper only when their members recognize that not everyone thinks or behaves similarly—nor should they be expected to. Diversity of views and perspectives is a prerequisite to problem solving, scientific and economic innovation, and artistic creativity. An appreciation of differ ent views is also an important factor in the development of domestic peace. Respect for diversity should be not only enshrined in Arab constitutions but codified in law and taught in educational institutions so that legal and cultural norms can harness the full potential of the different constituencies that form any Arab state.

The Arab uprisings demand that all regimes reconsider their policies toward the ethnic and religious constituencies that make up the Arab world. Inclusion is therefore a core component not only of political pluralism but also of social, geographic, and political cohesion in the region. Arab governments cannot hope to build prosperous societies unless they treat the entire population as citizens, irrespective of their ethnic, religious, or gender differences. The discourse of the emerging third forces must advocate a society that regards diversity as a positive force. It should also include an unwavering position that women are full participants in society, with equal political and legal rights.

Even after they take these three values to heart, the emerging third forces will still face fundamental challenges as they navigate a transitional period that will last years, if not decades. Standing in the way of the hope for a successful second Arab Awakening are the two dominant forces—existing governments or elites, and Islamists. Despite their shared history of not embracing pluralism, these two forces will also need to fight for real change and diversity.

Gradual Reform in Countries Not in Transition

To even attempt to follow a structured, gradual path, the countries that have not undergone regime change since 2011 must develop a transition that includes the existing leadership. In the best case, it would be led by regimes that have absorbed the idea that they can no longer hold on to absolute power and that keeping power means learning to share it. That process must start now.

While there are a few historic instances where such processes have been carried out by leaders, such as the political opening started by Mikhail Gorbachev in the Soviet Union, a gradual process with both regime leadership and broader participation offers the best chance of avoiding violent shocks to the systems. Such reform requires tremendous foresight by leaders who enjoy legitimacy and whose public will not spurn government overtures. As witnessed in Tunisia, Egypt, Libya, and Yemen, the point of no return in the Arab street is often reached sooner than anyone predicted. To avoid a street-led process of abrupt change, gradual change cannot move at a snail's pace or consist of ad hoc programs that never materialize into holistic, inclusive, measurable reform. Gradual must also mean concrete and sustained, delivering visible outcomes to the public.

So far, no Arab regime has put itself on a serious track to power sharing. Even in Morocco, which has done more in this regard than any other Arab country, the reforms have not brought any serious power sharing. The Islamist movement that won elections and formed the government appears to be totally deferential to the palace.

The Gulf states are acting as if their financial power will shield them forever from serious change. Ruling families in Saudi Arabia, Kuwait, Bahrain, Oman, and the United Arab Emirates have not internalized the needs of their populations—including migrant workers—for full stomachs and a serious share in running their country's affairs. It is unrealistic for these governments to assume that they can maintain this state of affairs forever. Yet many operate as if their power were perpetual. No financial or security arrangements can solve Bahrain's political crisis. Eventually the country must give the majority Shiite community its rightful share in decision making.

Regimes need to convince their populations that they are serious about reform. While different countries will follow different processes, there are shared elements that distinguish serious undertakings from mere window dressing. Reforms need to be inclusive, holistic, and measurable.

INCLUSIVE REFORM

In the past, reform in the Arab world was mostly nominal, imposed by the regime (often without consultation) and then hailed as a program that the bureaucracy could implement without question. More often than not, these regime-led reforms were insufficient, ad hoc, poorly communicated, and disingenuous. Without public participation, even the best intentions did not translate into effective programs.

These top-down reform projects have come in various guises. Some aimed at economic liberalization but were misleadingly called democratization efforts. They sometimes brought in dramatic economic changes and impressive growth, as happened in Tunisia and Egypt. But they did not alter the regimes' authoritarian character. They also lacked clear strategies for making growth more inclusive, so the economic benefits went largely to the business elite.

Other projects responded to social unrest and encompassed limited political reforms. For example, the National Action Charter of Bahrain, developed in 2001 in response to public demands for change, was written and implemented as a royal initiative without consultation with diverse social and political actors. Among the reforms were the creation of two parliamentary houses (one appointed and one elected) and the transformation of the country into a hereditary constitutional monarchy. In spite of their lofty stated goals, these programs delivered less-than-pluralizing reforms—the elected parliamentary house exercises no true legislative power, and the kingdom is not a real constitutional monarchy. The Bahraini public remains disillusioned and continues to demand change.

If reform projects concocted by the very leadership that needs reforming are to be seen as substantive and credible, they must adequately represent and empower all the major forces in society. When the military leaders in Egypt attempted to dictate the rules of the political game after Mubarak's fall, the rules were immediately rejected by the public.

HOLISTIC REFORM

Arab leaders have long argued that economic reform must precede political reform—so-called bread before freedom. Yet even when conducted in good faith, that strategy has failed to achieve either political or economic reform. Since necessary economic measures were carried out without the concomitant development of political oversight, abuses by economic actors went unchecked and unpunished. As a result, many economic reform programs benefited only a small elite. Even the potential economic impact of the reforms was hamstrung. It is difficult to encourage foreign investment if there is no independent press, parliament, or judicial system to address grievances and curtail corruption.

This means that a serious reform process must include political, economic, and cultural elements. It needs to be based in an understanding of how all aspects are linked so as to address these issues simultaneously.

MEASURABLE REFORM

Reform processes have often been long on promises and short on implementation. Clear performance indicators are necessary so that governments cannot get away with perfecting reform rhetoric without undertaking any reform.

At the Tunis Arab Summit in 2004, Arab leaders agreed on a reform document that reiterated their commitment, among other things, to "upholding justice and equality among all citizens; respecting human rights and the freedom of expression; ensuring the independence of the judiciary; pursuing the advancement of women in Arab society; acknowledging the role of civil society; and modernizing the education system." But they did not specify any performance indicators or evaluation mechanism to monitor progress. It is not surprising that these promises went largely unfulfilled.

None of the countries attempting a gradual reform process appears fully wedded to these principles. Reform from above in the Arab world is still moving too slowly—if at all—to keep up with the demands of a restless street. These regimes' commitment to pluralism has been largely rhetorical. They have not shied away from preaching inclusion to the Islamists while exercising exclusion. If these Arab regimes continue to ignore the urgent need for change, the street will catch up with them and they will have squandered the opportunity to lead their countries to stability and democracy.

Third forces have a critical role to play in helping their respective country's legitimate but increasingly contested rulers understand the urgency of engaging in this process. Regimes will have to abandon their sole dependency on their traditional constituencies, which are interested only in prolonging their own privileges, and shift alliances toward third forces as they become stronger and develop constituencies of their own. That requires the kind of farsightedness and calculated risk taking that Arab leaders so far have not shown.

Will Islamists Embrace Pluralism?

We can assume that, like all political forces, Islamists want to succeed. Whoever governs Arab countries will need to tackle tremendous political and economic problems. Islamists don't want to be blamed any more than other politicians for the mess. They know that they alone do not have economic answers and that jobs will not be created simply by repeating "Islam is the solution." Economic problem solving will come from detailed policies that encourage investment, attract tourism, create jobs, and reduce the public deficit.

Islamist parties need to offer such detailed proposals now. They have only recently turned their attention to these issues, so they will need to close the knowledge gap fast once they are partners—or leaders—in governments. They need to prove they can tackle such challenges effectively or they face being voted out. What they have offered so far are general platitudes that fall short of answering the huge problems facing their countries, all of which have been compounded by the loss of tourism, investment, and economic activity following the uprisings. Signs are also emerging that they may be making up for a lack of governing or economic experience by absorbing wholesale some of the bureaucratic and business elites from the old regimes, together with their practices.

If they want to be successful over the long term, the Islamists must practice what they preach. The emerging political systems in the Arab world must make it categorically clear that "no compulsion in religion" is not only a theological principle but also a political one. And whereas Islamic scholars may differ over whether this principle applies both ways in religion—meaning both to accepting Islam and to leaving it—there can be no such dispute in politics and governance. Arab societies cannot hope for constant renewal without a solid commitment to the peaceful rotation of power and the acceptance of the people's free will at all times.

Are Islamists embracing pluralism? While the positions of different Islamist parties in power today in Egypt, Tunisia, and Morocco have evolved toward moderation, their commitment to pluralism is still less than categorical. Further, the rise of the Salafis, though they are still a minority in these countries, is alarming. Their commitment to political pluralism is clearly absent, and on the street they regularly employ violence. It remains to be seen whether the peaceful majority of political Islamist forces will confront these groups, appease them, or even seek to use them in the competition for votes. This is a moment of truth for Islamist parties migrating toward pluralism. If there is a fight over who speaks for Islam, it must be led by the Islamists now in power in Egypt, Tunisia, and Morocco against those who insist on monopolizing the truth.

The inclusion of Islamists in the political systems does not absolve them from their obligations. Religious forces have to reconcile their ideologies with the fact that they are now political parties. When the two conflict, say, on women's rights, will they treat women as equal citizens or let their interpretation of religion dictate inferior treatment? They have not made this clear. The Muslim Brotherhood and at times even the Salafis have indicated their commitment to a civil state, but often with qualifications and without going into detail, leaving the impression that the promise is incomplete. Islamist forces want to win the public relations campaign to paint themselves as more pluralist than others, but their actions are not always convincing. Third forces in countries where Islamist parties have emerged can help by making it clear that they are for legitimate pluralism across the board and are not merely using popular terminology to exclude Islamists from the political arena.

Will Third Forces Rise to the Challenge?

Are the Arab world's two dominant forces redeemable? I have argued that both the "deep state" (the governing apparatus that is still in control, even where leaders have been overthrown) and the Islamists share one trait: a lack of a solid commitment to pluralism. It is possible that both might agree to an internal transformation in which they would moderate their views sufficiently to endorse democratic principles—possible, but unlikely. This is particularly true where regimes are still heavily invested in unaccountable, nontransparent systems. That they would endorse democracy and voluntarily agree to the peaceful rotation of power seems like a long shot. In most cases, they have lost the trust of their publics and face an uphill battle to regain it.

Islamists, on the other hand, are stymied to some degree by their intellectual proclivity for absolute, God-given truths and strict codes of personal behavior. Both the ruling elites and the Islamists have structured their organizations as compartmentalized, disciplined movements that were socially and economically self-sufficient, with membership often equating to a kind of fealty.

Perhaps hope still lies in the third forces, which at least have no record of abuse of power. They will have to go through a long, hard, disciplined process before they are able to not only challenge but hopefully assume power and contribute to a pluralistic society. In chapter 2 I discussed polls showing that Arab publics regard democracy as the best form of government, and that they understand what the concept means. In chapter 3 I also quoted polls demonstrating that most people in the Arab world do not want theocratic states, and that their vote for Islamists has been based on performance rather than on ideology. It follows, then, that Arab publics want their societies to be pluralistic, but they have not been able to evolve the proper political structures to achieve these objectives. Third forces will have to do just that. While these parties' evolution will differ in different countries, they all need to do specific things:

1) *Develop clear, detailed programs.* Most of the third forces emerging in the Arab world are defined more by what they are against than by what they are for. They are against old regimes, Islamists, or both. That will win them some temporary support, but it will not last long if they do not develop programs that define what they are for.

Beyond standing for pluralism, peaceful processes, and inclusion, they must address society's real economic and social needs, which is where most people's priorities lie. They need to send a message of hope, not fear. It needs to be developed after long consultations with their constituents rather than be written by a few experts. This unavoidably takes time: shortcuts will not achieve lasting results.

Further, while Arab political parties have been mainly ideological, advancing such visions as pan-Arabism, Baathism, or Islamism, the Arab public today faces more mundane challenges: jobs, economic mobility, equality before the law, the fight against corruption, and fairer and wider political representation. Third forces must address these issues through visions that are appealing to the public—not an easy feat. The new generation of leaders needs to be more fluent in pragmatic solutions than in dated ideological platforms.

2) *Build strong and coherent education policies.* Just as Arab countries need specific political, economic, and social programs, they also need education policies that promote pluralism, tolerance, respect for different points of view, and critical thinking. Third forces need to be ardent advocates for policies that prepare the next generation to be true citizens, rather than subjects, at a very early age.

3) *Work from the base up.* Most political parties in the Arab world have been created by elites who tend to register parties first and look for constituencies later. Islamists have succeeded because they had real connections with people, developed over decades of providing health, education, and other services that inefficient or corrupt state systems failed to deliver. Third forces must build up their base, resisting the temptation to register parties before they are ready.

This is particularly true in states that have not undergone transition, where some time is still available. Regimes in these countries will not listen to third forces unless they have independent constituent support. In other countries, such as Egypt and Tunisia, third forces will have to face the challenge of building up their base while fighting for space against the organized Islamist forces. Political organizing is a science that cannot be done haphazardly. Third forces must learn how to build networks, party structures, and mobilization efforts.

4) *Develop financial resources.* Third forces lack the

vast resources of the state and the Islamists, who rely on both domestic and foreign sources of funding. This will remain an obstacle unless they develop effective means of collecting small donations from regular citizens (the Internet can be very helpful) as well as larger sums from more affluent representatives of the private sector.

In countries that have not undergone transitions, third forces need to invest time and energy in convincing the private sector that a stable business environment and supportive legal regime can be achieved in a real democracy. It should be increasingly clear to the business community that its reflexive support of autocratic regimes will no longer bring it the stability it needs. The Arab private sector has been closely linked to governments, but as corrupt leaders fall its interests are being hurt. Turkey has achieved prosperity partially because its private sector managed to become independent of government. The same effort must be made in the Arab world. The vibrancy, innovation, and youth of the Arab start-up community bode well for success.

5) *Promote programs, not individuals.* Personality cults dominate both the Arab political elite and other secular forces. Hamdeen Sabahi, Amr Moussa, and Abdel Munim Abul-Foutouh, for example, each received millions of votes in the June 2012 Egyptian presidential elections, largely because of their widespread name recognition rather than their support of any detailed spe-

cific programs. Such popular support cannot be expected in the long term if these individuals cannot develop programs with which people identify. It will take some time for the tendency toward patriarchal structures to be overcome.

6) *Consolidate forces.* It is easy for individuals or forces to think they have all the answers to their country's problems and consequently form parties and run for parliament. However, this situation leads to the proliferation of individual parties, and none of which would have much effect on its own. For example, 116 parties contested the parliamentary elections in Tunisia in October 2011, scattering the secular vote and allowing the unified Islamists to win around 40 percent of the seats. Only a handful of parties won a significant number of seats.

There must be a move to consolidate forces. This is already taking place in Egypt and Tunisia, resulting in a more level playing field. Spain had a similar experience in the mid-1970s. Its first post-Franco elections were contested by 161 parties, but only 7 got more than one representative elected to parliament. Most disappeared as the country's democracy matured.

Absolute purity of ideology within each party must also be abandoned. Parties need to agree on general principles but allow varying points of view to avoid undue fragmentation.

7) *Be patient.* None of this will develop quickly or easily. Many parties will fail, and others will face insurmountable difficulties. Only the commit-

ted and patient will ultimately flourish. Their
success will be the result of credible programs,
strong organizational capabilities, sound financial
resources, and proven ability to deliver desired
changes. Those who are in it for the glory, who
look for shortcuts, or who rely on slogans or
elitist platforms will soon disappear. The field
will be left to those who are truly committed to
pluralism and who also understand that they
themselves may not reap many benefits in their
lifetimes.

Third forces will take years or even decades
to emerge as credible alternatives. But emerge
they must if the Arab world is to have any chance
for a bright future.

This fight to fashion viable and vibrant
third forces is one that the new generation must
embrace. They will have to overcome difficult
obstacles. The biggest one will be how to build
political structures and a culture that regard diversity and pluralism as necessary for prosperity
and stability. They will also need to confront the
two formidable forces that are driven more by
their own interests than by the common good
and inherently less committed (if not opposed)
to entertaining differing points of view.

Shortly after the start of the Arab uprisings in Egypt, Lisa
Anderson, the president of the American University in Cairo,
gave a talk at the Carnegie Endowment for International Peace
in Washington. She observed that "this new generation is not
revolting *against* their parents, but *on behalf* of them." It is in-

deed up to the new generation in the Arab world not to accept what their parents accepted. Achieving this will take commitment, perseverance, wisdom, and patience, the latter two being traits that the young often lack.

Some will read this book and regard its arguments as a naive, almost romantic view of an Arab world that does not exist, a mirage in the desert, totally detached from reality. They will point out the current tumultuous state of affairs, and wonder how one can ever talk about diversity and tolerance when Syria is being dismantled before our eyes—as political grievances shared across the region turn sectarian, pitting one neighbor against another in a zero-sum battle for survival. How can one dream of a democratic Arab world when countries such as Iraq and Lebanon are still organized along sectarian and not national lines, often clashing with each other violently. How can one even speak of an awakening, many will argue, when the initial calls for dignity and good governance have turned into an Islamist takeover by forces whose idea of reform is to take all steps necessary to ensure their grip on power as they slowly oblige the whole of society to practice what only they believe? How can one mention tolerance when Salafist movements openly reject democratic norms and have often resorted to using violence to advance their views?

Status quo forces in the Arab world will point to the past three years and say, "We told you so." They will argue that the turmoil that has characterized most of the transitions since 2011 is evidence that their policies of imposed stability have worked better even if the political space is limited or closed. They will dismiss arguments that much of what we witness today is in fact a direct result of their own policies of suppressing the development of societies that respect diversity in all its forms and that empower people to exercise a true sense of citizenship. They will, in most cases, ignore lessons from history, each group believing that it is the exception to these patterns we have seen. They have learned nothing, and, in their hopeless stand against the wheels of history, their influence and power can only wane over time.

Many in the West have already written off the Arab world, refusing once again to view this region in any way other than in black and white terms—mostly in black. After romantically expecting the region to turn to democratic norms instantly, most now can see only the rise of Islamist forces, exclusionist discourses, and violence across this region.

It might be too much to expect people to have a historical perspective of what has transpired since 2011. Most people's attention spans are short, their patience even more so. Internalizing the argument that historic transformations take time—they always have, everywhere on earth—is difficult, particularly in today's high-velocity culture. Few have time for historical arguments or analytical explanations.

I strongly believe, however, that history is our guiding light on what is transpiring in today's Arab Awakenings. I write not out of a romantic connection to the region, but rather out of a firm conviction that the battle of ideas has finally started to unfold in the contemporary Arab world. It is a battle that will be won only by those who are ready to toil and sweat to get their point of view acknowledged. Some emerging political forces, frustrated by not being able to build national organizations and political programs, may advocate undemocratic means, as they have already, to stem the tide of Islamists. They, too, will fade.

The Arab world will go through a period of turmoil in which exclusionist forces will attempt to dominate the landscape with absolute truths and new dictatorships. These forces will also fade, because in the end, exclusionist, authoritarian discourses cannot answer the people's need for a better quality of life—economically, politically, culturally, and otherwise. As history has demonstrated overwhelmingly, where there is respect for diversity, there is prosperity. Contrary to what Arab societies have been taught for decades by their governments to believe—that tolerance, acceptance of different points of view, and critical thinking are destructive to national unity and economic growth—experience proves that societies cannot keep renewing themselves and thereby thrive except through diversity. Neither the theological Iranian model of Wilayat-al-Faqih nor the secular, authoritarian model of the Mubarak regime has succeeded in solving the region's economic, political, or cultural challenges.

But this realization will not come automatically, or quickly. The Arab world will witness many attempts by religious and secular forces to dominate the emerging landscapes in this region. Mistakes will be made, and there will be more struggles. The realization that salvation will come through diversity, coexistence, and a new mind-set that finally recognizes the beauty—and strength—of differences will not be automatic. It will require dedicated and sustained work on the ground for decades to come. It needs generations of believers to articulate such views, to build a sense of true citizenship, and to develop innovative and indigenous mechanisms for protecting that Arab citizenship, alongside programs that address people's needs, all the while embracing inclusive discourses and defending different outlooks.

This task is not for the fainthearted or those whom I consider to be the "true" romantics—individuals who are too quick to give up if democracy does not emerge overnight, or if their lifestyles are not guaranteed without them rolling up their sleeves. This job will require leadership, vision, and, most important, decades of hard work. There are no shortcuts to democracy or prosperity.

This is how I see the true contribution of this book. It is not, by any means, a panacea to the region's complex reality. My hope is that, as it is read and reread through the lens of time, twenty, thirty, or fifty years down the line, and possibly after all other alternatives to diversity have been exhausted, it will inspire some to reject the prospect of waiting that long, and to encourage them to devote their energies to creating a pluralistic Arab world now that the chance to do so is at least made possible through the historic process just unleashed.

The second Arab Awakening has just begun, and the end may not be known in this generation's lifetime. But this is a battle worth waging and winning—the battle for pluralism across the Arab world.

Notes

1.
The First Arab Awakening

1. George Antonius, *The Arab Awakening: The Story of the Arab National Movement* (Philadelphia: J. B. Lippencott, 1939).

2. That phrase has been scanned from Antonius's original book and included as an epigraph in this book.

3. Albert Hourani, *Arabic Thought in the Liberal Age: 1798–1939* (Oxford: Oxford University Press, 1962).

2.
Redefining Arab Moderation

1. "2009 Annual Arab Public Opinion Survey," University of Maryland & Zogby International, April–May 2009, http://www.brookings.edu/~/media/events/2009/5/19%20arab%20opinion/2009_arab_public_opinion_poll.pdf.

2. James Zogby, "Arab Attitudes Towards Syria, 2011," Arab American Institute Foundation, September–October 2011, http://aai.3cdn.net/c3bd 1500d778d87ac7_ism6b92b1.pdf.

3. For a detailed discussion of how Arabs and Muslim view democracy, see John L. Esposito and Dalia Mogahed, *Who Speaks for Islam? What a Billion Muslims Really Think* (New York: Gallup Press, 2007).

4. "Corruption Perceptions Index 2011," Transparency International, 2011, http://cpi.transparency.org/cpi2011/results/.

5. For a discussion of such a rentier system in Jordan, see Marwan Muasher, "A Decade of Struggling Reform Efforts in Jordan: The Resilience of the Rentier System," (Washington, DC: Carnegie Endowment for International Peace, May 2011).

6. Klaus Schwab, "The Global Competitiveness Report 2010–2011," World Economic Forum, http://www3.weforum.org/docs/WEF_GlobalCom petitivenessReport_2010–11.pdf.

7. "Arab American Physicians," National Arab American Medical Association, http://www.naama.com/naama-arab-american-physicians.php.

8. Bertelsmann Stiftung, "BTI 2012 Tunisia Country Report," http://www.bti-project.de/fileadmin/Inhalte/reports/2012/pdf/BTI%202012%20 Tunisia.pdf.

9. See *Arab Human Development Report 2002: Creating Opportunities for Future Generations,* United Nations Development Programme, http://www.arab-hdr.org/publications/other/ahdr/ahdr2002e.pdf.

10. "Egypt Conflict Alert," International Crisis Group, February 4, 2013, http://www.crisisgroup.org/en/publication-type/alerts/2013/egypt-conflict -alert.aspx.

11. Michael J. Totten, "US Criticized by Tunisian Secularists for Backing Islamists," *World Affairs,* March 12, 2012 http://www.worldaffairsjour nal.org/blog/michael-j-totten/us-criticized-tunisian-secularists-backing -islamists.

3.
Islamist Movements

Parts of this chapter have been written with Dalia Mogahed, co-author with John L. Esposito of *Who Speaks for Islam? What a Billion Muslims Really Think* (New York: Gallup Press, 2007).

1. Djerejian described this "objective" of Islamists in a speech he delivered at the Meridien House, June 4, 1992.

2. In my earlier book *The Arab Center* I attempted to classify political Islam into three main groups, and I am largely reproducing that classification here. I have now added a fourth category to that list, the Salafis, who recently gained prominence after emerging as a strong political force during the 2011 Egyptian parliamentary elections.

3. Hamas, itself an offshoot of the Muslim Brotherhood, is probably the only exception to groups affiliated with the Muslim Brotherhood that have not renounced violence as a result of the Israeli occupation.

4. BBC, "Profile: Egypt's Muslim Brotherhood," June 26, 2012, http://www.bbc.co.uk/news/world-middle-east-12313405.

5. Sana Abed-Kotob, "The Accommodationists Speak: Goals and Strategies of the Muslim Brotherhood in Egypt," *International Journal of Middle East Studies* 27, no.3 (1995): 328.

6. The Holy Quran 2:256.

7. This is the opinion of the highly regarded Sunni scholar Yusuf al-Qaradawi. Read more at http://qaradawi.net/component/content/article/46/1972.html.

8. For a detailed analysis of the Muslim Brotherhood in Egypt and the group's participation in the political process, see Nathan J. Brown and Amr Hamzawy, "Between Religion and Politics" (Washington, DC: Carnegie Endowment for International Peace, 2010), 9–46.

9. That parliament was deemed unconstitutional by the Constitutional Court and dissolved by the military council in June 2012.

10. For the full text of the platform, see: http://www.hurryh.com/Party_Program.aspx (Arabic).

11. This is an unpublished national Gallup survey conducted in Egypt in February 2012 and analyzed specifically for this chapter.

12. Ibid.

13. For a detailed discussion of the economic agendas of the PJF as well as Islamist parties in Morocco, Tunisia, and Jordan, see Ibrahim Saif and Muhammad Abu Rumman, "The Economic Agenda of the Islamist Parties," Carnegie Endowment for International Peace, May 2012, http://carnegieendowment.org/2012/05/29/economic-agenda-of-islamist-parties/bofh.

14. Nathan J. Brown and Amr Hamzawy, "Between Religion and Politics" (Washington, DC: Carnegie Endowment for International Peace, 2010).

15. Dalia Mogahed, "Tracking the Revolutionary Mood," *Foreign Policy*, January 24, 2012, http://www.foreignpolicy.com/articles/2012/01/24/The_State_of_Egypt.

16. It is unfortunate that most of these are in Arabic and thus not known to many in the West

17. Rached Al-Ghannouchi, *Huquq al-Muwatanah*, (Tunis. Matba'at Tunis Qarthaj, 1989), 39–43.

18. Rached Ghannouchi, interview by author, Washington, DC, December 1, 2011.

19. Islamopedia Online, "Tunisia's Rached Ghannouchi on Secularism," March 10, 2012, http://www.islamopediaonline.org/news/tunisias-rached-ghannouchis-secularism.

20. Sana Ajmi, "Discriminatory Qualifications for Tunisia's President Cause Controversy," Tunisia-live.net, December 11, 2011, http://www.tunisia-live.net/2011/12/11/discriminatory-qualifications-for-tunisias-president-cause-controversy/.

21. This is an unpublished national Gallup survey conducted in Tunisia in spring 2010 and analyzed specifically for this chapter.

22. Ibid.

23. For a detailed account of the history and political participation of the PJD in the Moroccan political process, see Nathan J. Brown and Amr Hamzawy, *Between Religion and Politics* (Washington, DC: Carnegie Endowment for International Peace, 2010), 79–104.

24. www.pjd.ma/sites/default/files/SG_11_Balagh_R%C3%A9forme_con stiutlle_100311.pdf (Arabic).

25. For more on the PJD's economic program, see Ibrahim Saif and Muhammad Abu Rumman, "The Economic Agenda of the Islamist Parties," Carnegie Endowment for International Peace, May 2012.

26. Al Quds Center, "The Platform of the Islamic Action Front Party," 7th ed., 2, www.alqudscenter.com/uploads/Jabha.pdf.

27. See, for example, Janine Clark, "Women in Islamist Parties: The Case of Jordan's Islamic Action Front," SADA, July 20, 2004, http://carnegie endowment.org/2008/08/20/women-in-islamist-parties-case-of-jordan-s -islamic-action-front/6ccf.

28. John L. Esposito and Dalia Mogahed, *Who Speaks for Islam? What a Billion Muslims Really Think* (New York: Gallup Press, 2007).

29. Some examples include: "Their political system is transparent and they are following democracy in its true sense," according to one Egyptian respondent. "Liberty and freedom and being open minded with each other," said another Tunisian respondent. For more information see Esposito and Mogahed, *Who Speaks for Islam?*

30. Mohamed Younis and Ahmed Younis, "Support for Islamists Declines as Egypt's Election Nears," Gallup, May 18, 2012, http://www.gallup .com/poll/154706/Support-Islamists-Declines-Egypt-Election-Nears.aspx. As Tables 4 and 5 indicate below, this research also shows declining public confidence in the Egyptian parliament when it comes to appointing a prime minister and deciding who will write a new constitution.

Table 4. Polling responses of Egyptian adults regarding the appointment of a prime minister.

Should the next prime minister of Egypt be appointed by _____?		
	February 2012	April 2012
The party that wins the most seats in the parliament	46%	27%
The ruling military council	13%	12%
The newly elected president next summer	27%	44%

Source: Mohamed Younis and Ahmed Younis, "Support for Islamists Declines as Egypt's Election Nears," Gallup, May 18, 2012, http://www.gallup.com/poll/154706/Support-Islamists-Declines -Egypt-Election-Nears.aspx.

Table 5. Polling responses of Egyptian adults regarding the selection of individuals to write a new constitution.

Would you rather those writing Egypt's new constitution be chosen by _____?

	February 2012	April 2012
The party that wins the most seats in the parliament	62%	44%
The ruling military council	14%	17%
The newly elected president next summer	9%	14%

Source: Mohamed Younis and Ahmed Younis, "Support for Islamists Declines as Egypt's Election Nears," Gallup, May 18, 2012, http://www.gallup.com/poll/154706/Support-Islamists-Declines-Egypt-Election-Nears.aspx.

31. Ibid.

32. Ibid.

33. Jeffrey M. Jones, "US Satisfaction Slips Slightly to 20%," Gallup, June 13, 2012, http://www.gallup.com/poll/155162/Satisfaction-Slips-Slightly.aspx.

34. Mogahed, "Tracking the Revolutionary Mood."

35. Ibid.

36. "After the Arab Uprisings: Women on Rights, Religion, and Rebuilding," Gallup, summer 2012, http://www.gallup.com/poll/155306/Arab-Uprisings-Women-Rights-Religion-Rebuilding.aspx.

37. Jay Loschky, "Gallup Releases New Findings on Women's Rights After the Arab Uprisings," Gallup, June 25, 2012, http://thegallupblog.gallup.com/2012/06/gallup-releases-new-findings-on-womens.html.

38. Ibid.

39. Mogahed, "Tracking the Revolutionary Mood."

40. Heba Saleh, "Egyptian Rulers Face Showdown with Islamists," *Financial Times,* November 2, 2011, http://www.ft.com/intl/cms/s/0/d621a9c8-0576-11e1-a429-0044feabdco.html#axzz25nfBheyL.

41. For more on such positions, see Amira Nowaira, "Egypt's Muslim Brotherhood Continues to Alienate Itself from Its People," *Guardian,* November 25, 2011, http://www.guardian.co.uk/commentisfree/2011/nov/25/egypt-muslim-brotherhood-alienate-people.

42. Palestinian Center for Policy and Survey Research, "Poll November 19," March 16–18, 2006, http://www.pcpsr.org/survey/polls/2006/p19e.pdf.

43. Ahmed Younis, "More Egyptians Find It Difficult to Make Ends Meet," *Gallup World,* October 27, 2011, http://www.gallup.com/poll/150356/Egyptians-Finding-Difficult-Ends-Meet.aspx.

44. Mogahed, "Tracking the Revolutionary Mood."

4.
Assessing What Has Changed

1. For a comprehensive discussion about the difficulties emerging political parties face in new democracies, see Thomas Carothers, *Confronting
the Weakest Link: Aiding Political Parties in New Democracies* (Washington,
DC: Carnegie Endowment for International Peace, 2006).

2. International Monetary Fund, "Middle East and North Africa:
Economic Outlook and Key Challenges," Deauville Partnership Ministerial
Meeting, April 20, 2012, Washington, DC.

3. "Tunisia: Investigate Attacks by Religious Extremists," Human
Rights Watch, October 15, 2012, http://www.hrw.org/news/2012/10/15/tunisia
-investigate-attacks-religious-extremists-0.

4. See Egyptian State Information Service website, http://www.sis.gov
.eg/En/Story.aspx?sid=56424. Translation was not altered unless the meaning was obviously unclear.

5. Abdel Ghaffour, interview by author, Cairo, Egypt, June 10, 2012.

6. Frederic Wehrey, "The Precarious Ally: Bahrain's Impasse and U.S.
Policy," Carnegie Endowment for International Peace, February 2013.

7. Frederic Wehrey, *Sectarian Politics in the Gulf: From the Iraq War to
the Arab Uprisings,* (Columbia University Press, forthcoming).

8. "Interview with Syrian President Bashar al-Assad," *Wall Street Journal,* January 31, 2011, http://online.wsj.com/article/SB10001424052748703833
2045761147121441122894.html.

9. One can argue that the Iraqi case of acknowledging the rights of Iraqi
Kurds was somewhat forced by the United States after the war on Iraq in 2003.

10. For a detailed discussion on the performance of the PJD, see Marina Ottaway, "Morocco: Can the Third Way Succeed," Carnegie Endowment for International Peace, July 31, 2012, http://www.carnegieendowment
.org/2012/07/31/morocco-can-third-way-succeed/d30p.

11. For a detailed discussion of the National Agenda, see Marwan
Muasher, *The Arab Center: The Promise of Moderation* (New Haven: Yale
University Press, 2008), 246–53.

12. Marwan Muasher, "A Decade of Struggling Reform Efforts in Jordan: The Resilience of the Rentier System," Carnegie Endowment for International Peace, May 2011, http://carnegieendowment.org/2011/05/11/decade
-of-struggling-reform-efforts-in-jordan-resilience-of-rentier-system/1gf.

13. Marina Ottaway and Marwan Muasher, "Arab Monarchies: Chance
for Reform, Yet Unmet," Carnegie Endowment for International Peace, December 2011, http://www.carnegieendowment.org/2011/12/16/arab-monar
chies-chance-for-reform-yet-unmet/bkm6.

14. Ibid.

15. The one-man-one-vote formula in Jordan is a misnomer, as it suggests a fair system used in many countries around the world. In the Jordanian case, the number of districts does not match the number of seats, with all districts consisting of an unequal number of seats. Voters are allowed to cast one vote in their districts, even though several candidates are elected from that district corresponding to the number of seats it has. This, together with the gerrymandering of districts, has produced unrepresentative parliaments, favoring tribal elites and local notables, who are traditionally dependent on services from the state, while discouraging the formation of political parties.

16. Center for Strategic Studies, "Ma ba'd al-intikhabat al-niyabiyyah wa ba'dh al-qadaya ar-rahina," University of Jordan, February 2013, http:// www.jcss.org/ShowNewsAr.aspx?NewsId=297#.US52TVtnWpA.

17. Rhayyel Gharaibeh, interview by author, Amman, Jordan, August 7, 2012.

5.
Education for Pluralism

Parts of this chapter have been written with Muhammad Faour, who is leading an Education for Citizenship Initiative at the Carnegie Middle East Center in Beirut. Parts of the chapter have already been published. See Muhammad Faour and Marwan Muasher, *Education for Citizenship in the Arab World: Key to the Future*, Carnegie Endowment for International Peace, October 2011, http://carnegieendowment.org/files/citizenship_educa tion.pdf.

1. Muhammad Faour and Marwan Muasher, *Education for Citizenship in the Arab World: Key to the Future*, Carnegie Endowment for International Peace, October 2011, http://carnegieendowment.org/files/citizenship_educa tion.pdf, 4.

2. Marwan Muasher, "The Arab World in Crisis: Redefining Arab Moderation," Carnegie Endowment for International Peace, January 2011, http://carnegieendowment.org/2011/01/27/arab-world-in-crisis-redefining -arab-moderation/p4d.

3. Nabih Maroun and Hatem Samman, "How to Succeed at Education Reform: The Case for Saudi Arabia and the Broader GCC Region," *Booz Allen Hamilton* (2008): 18.

4. Albert Hourani, *Arabic Thought in the Liberal Age 1798–1939* (Cambridge: Cambridge University Press, 2009), 130–47.

5. Roxanne L. Euben and Muhammad Qasim Zaman, eds., *Princeton Readings in Islamist Thought* (Princeton: Princeton University Press, 2009), 7.

6. Nasr Hamid Abu Zayd, *Reformation of Islamic Thought: A Critical Historical Analysis* (Amsterdam: Amsterdam University Press, 2006), 37.

7. Ibid., 40.

8. Euben and Zaman, *Princeton Readings in Islamist Thought*, 53.

9. Abu Zayd, *Reformation of Islamic Thought*, 37.

10. Justin Yifu Lin, "Youth Bulge: A Democratic Dividend or a Demographic Bomb in Developing Countries?" *World Bank*, January 5, 2012, http://blogs.worldbank.org/developmenttalk/node/693.

11. World Bank, *Recovering from the Crisis: Middle East and North Africa Region—A Regional Economic Update*, April 2010, http://www-wds.worldbank.org/external/default/WDSContentServer/WDSP/IB/2010/07/07/000333037_20100707003731/Rendered/PDF/545110WP0REPLA1risisopubo5112110web.pdf, 15.

12. As cited in Khawla Khanekah, "Citizenship Education in Iraq," Carnegie Middle East Center, May 2012, 10.

13. Egypt Ministry of Education, "National Education" (Arabic), Grade 11, 2008, 30.

14. Ryuichi Funatsu, "Al-Kawakibi's Thesis and Its Echoes in the Arab World Today," *Harvard Middle Eastern and Islamic Review* 7 (2006): 12–14.

15. Hourani, *Arabic Thought in the Liberal Age 1798–1939*, 335–38.

16. Bahrain Ministry of Education, "Education for Citizenship" (Arabic), Grade 4, 43–46.

17. Organization for Economic Cooperation and Development, *Education at a Glance, 2004*, 2004, http://www.oecd.org/dataoecd/35/34/33714562.pdf, 4.

18. UNESCO Institute for Statistics, *Global Education Digest 2011*, 2011, http://www.uis.unesco.org/Library/Documents/global_education_digest_2011_en.pdf, 10.

19. Ibid., 16.

20. UNESCO Institute for Statistics, *World Atlas of Gender Equality in Education*, 2012, http://www.uis.unesco.org/Education/Documents/unesco-world-atlas-gender-education-2012.pdf, 76.

21. Ibid., 28, and UNESCO Institute for Statistics, *Global Education Digest*, 10.

22. UNESCO Institute for Statistics, *World Atlas of Gender Equality in Education*, 92.

23. Six Arab countries participated in the 2003 TIMSS as compared to fourteen countries in the 2007 and 2011 TIMSS. In the 2006 PIRLS, only

three Arab countries participated, as opposed to six who participated in 2011. TIMSS and PIRLS results by country are available at timss.bc.edu.

24. Only four Arab countries participated in the 2009 PISA test. PISA results by country are available at www.oecd.org/pisa.

25. UNESCO, *Regional Overview: Arab States, EFA Global Monitoring Report 2011: The Hidden Crisis: Armed Conflict and Education*, 2011, http:// unesdoc.unesco.org/images/0019/001907/190743e.pdf, 6.

26. *Arab Human Development Report 2003: Building a Knowledge Society*, United Nations Development Programme, 2003, http://hdr.undp.org/ en/reports/regionalreports/arabstates/RBAS_ahdr2003_EN.pdf, 6.

27. For math and science results see I. V. S. Mullis, M. O. Martin, and P. Foy (with J. F. Olson, C. Preuschoff, E. Erberber, A. Arora, and J. Galia, *TIMSS 2007 International Mathematics Report: Findings from IEA's Trends in International Mathematics and Science Study at the Fourth and Eighth Grades* (Chestnut Hill, MA: TIMSS & PIRLS International Study Center, 2008).

28. Kevin Watkins, "Education Failures Fan the Flames in the Arab World," World Education Blog, February 23, 2011, http://efareport.wordpress .com/2011/02/23/education-failures-fan-the-flames-in-the-arab-world/.

29. *The Road Not Traveled: Education Reform in the Middle East and North Africa* (Washington, DC: World Bank, 2008), 88.

30. Kamal Naguib, "The Production and Reproduction of Culture in Egyptian Schools," in *Cultures of Arab Schooling: Critical Ethnographies from Egypt*, ed. Linda Herrera and Carlos Alberto Torres (New York: State University of New York Press, 2006), 68.

31. Judith Cochran, *Democracy in the Middle East: The Impact of Religion and Education* (Lanham: Lexington, 2011), 120.

32. *Arab Human Development Report 2003: Building a Knowledge Society*, 54.

33. Cochran, *Democracy in the Middle East*, 120.

34. Eleanor Abdella Doumato, "Saudi Arabia: From 'Wahhabi' Roots to Contemporary Revisionism," in *Teaching Islam: Textbooks and Religion in the Middle East*, ed. Eleanor Abdella Doumato and Gregory Starrett (Boulder: Lynne Rienner, 2011), 154.

35. Ibid., 156.

36. Elham Abdul-Hameed, "Egyptian Education and Citizenship Culture: Status and Expectations," (Arabic), Carnegie Middle East Center, December 2011, 4–5; *Arab Human Development Report 2003: Building a Knowledge Society*, 53.

37. Mustafa Qasim, *Education and Citizenship* (Arabic) (Cairo: Cairo Institute for Human Rights, 2006); Pakinaz Baraka, "Citizenship Education

in Egyptian Public Schools, What Values to Teach and in Which Administrative and Political Contexts," *Journal of Education for International Development* 3, no. 3 (2007); N. Ayed et al., "Education, diversité et cohésion sociale en Tunisie," in *Education, diversité et cohésion sociale en Méditerranée occidentale*, ed. S. Tawil et al. (Rabat: UNESCO, 2010).

38. Ibid., 306–7.

39. Qasim, *Education and Citizenship* 150–51; Abdul-Hameed, "Egyptian Education and Citizenship Culture," 5.

40. Baraka, "Citizenship Education in Egyptian Public Schools," 11.

41. Ibid.

42. From a presentation by Abdullah Abdussalam, Ministry of Education, Libya, at the expert group meeting on religious identity and citizenship education, Carnegie Middle East Center, Beirut, Lebanon, March 8, 2012.

43. Saif Al-Maamari, "Citizenship Education in Bahrain" (Arabic), Carnegie Middle East Center, March 2012, 6, 9, 10; "Citizenship Education in the UAE" (Arabic), Carnegie Middle East Center, March 2012, 7, 9; and "Citizenship Education in Oman" (Arabic), Carnegie Middle East Center March 2012, 9, 11, 13–15.

44. Ahmed Al-Hadhiri, "Citizenship Education in Morocco" (Arabic), Carnegie Middle East Center, June 2012, 9.

45. Muhyieddeen Touq, "Citizenship Education in Jordan and Palestine" (Arabic), Carnegie Middle East Center, March 2012, 35.

46. Al-Imran sura, verse 85. This verse and other related verses are explained in the eighth-grade textbook, first term (2010–11), 22.

47. For more information on Egypt, see Ragaey Nasri, "The Case of Egypt in Light of Previous Experiences," Expert Group Meeting on Religious Identity and Citizenship Education in the Arab Countries, *Carnegie Middle East Center*, Beirut, March 8, 2012. Further information on Egypt was given during that meeting by Elham Abdul-Hameed and Ahmad Al-Halawany, and on Lebanon by Salim Daccache, Hisham Nashabeh, and Ghassan Hublus.

48. Muhammad Faour, "Citizenship and Religious Identity: Issues Beyond Laws" (Arabic), *Annahar* (December 9, 2011).

49. Elie Elhadj, "Syria's Islamic Textbooks Teach Political Indoctrination and Intolerance," *Middle East Review of International Affairs* 15, no. 2 (June 2011): 63.

50. Ibid., 64.

51. These countries include Jordan, Lebanon, and all six Gulf Cooperation Council countries. See Saif Al-Maamari, "Citizenship Education in the Arab Gulf Countries: Challenges and Horizons" (Arabic), Carnegie Middle East Center, March 2012, 5.

52. *The Road Not Traveled: Education Reform in the Middle East and North Africa* (Washington, DC: World Bank, 2008): 95, 292, 308 table A.1.

53. Ibid., table A.2.

54. Mourad Ezzine, "Education in the Arab World: Shift to Quality in Math, Science & Technology Faltering," *MENA Knowledge and Learning*, no. 2 (February 2009): 1, http://siteresources.worldbank.org/INTMENA/News%20and%20Events/22073700/QuickNote_2.pdf.

55. Touq, "Citizenship Education in Jordan and Palestine," 44, 60.

56. Nemer Frayha, "Citizenship Education in Lebanon" (Arabic), Carnegie Middle East Center, March 2012, 26, 30.

57. UNESCO, "Education Policies and Strategies 14," *Global Synthesis of the Findings of UNESS Documents: Progress Report (Working Document)* (April 2009), 12, 23, 30; G. Gonzalez et al., *Lessons from the Field: Developing and Implementing the Qatar Student Assessment System, 2002–2006*, 2009, http://www.rand.org/content/dam/rand/pubs/technical_reports/2009/RAND_TR620.sum.pdf, 26.

58. *Arab Human Development Report 2003: Building a Knowledge Society*, 165–75.

59. Ibid., 40.

60. For studies on the impact of contextual variables on student achievement in math and sciences see, for example, Murad Jurdak, "The Impact of Contextual Variables on Science Achievement in the Arab Countries: Results from TIMSS 2003," in *The World of Science Education: Arab States*, ed. S. BouJaoude and Z. Dagher (Rotterdam: Sense Publishers, 2009), 27–40; Theresa M. Akey, "School Context, Student Attitudes and Behavior, and Academic Achievement: An Exploratory Analysis," MDRC, January 2006, www.mdrc.org/publications/419/full.pdf; Janet C. Quint, Theresa M. Akey, Shelley Rappaport, and Cynthia Willner, "Instructional Leadership, Teaching Quality, and Student Achievement: Suggestive Evidence from Three Urban School Districts," MDRC, December 2007, www.mdrc.org/publications/470/print.html.

61. See, for example, *The Progress of Education Reform* 11, no. 5 (October 2010): 3, www.ecs.org/per; Wolfram Schulz et al., *ICCS 2009 International Report: Civic Knowledge, Attitudes, and Engagement Among Lower Secondary Students in 38 Countries*, IEA, 2009, http//www.iea.nl, 251; Kaya Yilmaz, "Learner-Centered Instruction as a Means to Realise Democratic Education: The Problems and Constraints Confronting Learner-Centered Instruction in Turkey," *Studies in Learning, Evaluation, Innovation and Development* 4, no. 3 (December 2007): 15–28.

62. See, for example, "School Climate Research Summary," *Center for Social and Emotional Education*, 2007, http://nscc.csee.net/effective/school_

climate_research_summary.pdf; J. Cohen, "Social, Emotional, Ethical, and Academic Education: Creating a Climate for Learning, Participation in Democracy, and Well-Being," *Harvard Educational Review* 76, no. 2 (2006): 201–37; J. Cohen, L. McCabe, N. M. Michelli, and T. Pickeral, "School Climate: Research, Policy, Practice, and Teacher Education," *Teachers College Record*, forthcoming.

63. Jonathan Cohen, Terry Pickeral, and Molly McCloskey, "The Challenge of Assessing School Climate," *Educational Leadership* 66, no. 4 (December 2008/January 2009), www.ascd.org/publications/educational-leadership/dec08/vol66/num04/The-Challenge-of-Assessing-School-Climate.aspx.

6.
The Second Arab Awakening and the Arab-Israeli Conflict

1. Shlomo Ben Ami would later become the foreign minister during the Camp David talks and the Taba talks of 2000–2001.

2. Marwan Muasher, "Palestinian-Israeli Direct Talks: The Case for a Regional Approach," Carnegie Endowment for International Peace, August 2010, http://carnegieendowment.org/2010/08/24/palestinian-israeli-direct-talks-case-for-regional-approach/bly7.

3. Ali Abunimah, "Palestinians on the Verge of a Majority: Population and Politics in Palestine-Israel," *Jerusalem Fund*, May 12, 2008, http://www.thejerusalemfund.org/ht/display/ContentDetails/i/2244.

4. See, for example, Zogby Research Services, "Afghanistan, Political Concerns, Iraq, Social Media," reprinted with permission by the Arab American Institute Foundation, November 2011.

5. Tom Friedman, "B.E., Before Egypt. A.E., After Egypt," *New York Times*, February 1, 2011.

6. "Negotiator in Chief" (Tzipi Livni interview with Walter Isaacson), *Aspen Idea*, Winter 2011/2012, http://www.scribd.com/doc/73060086/Aspen-Winter-11-12-Issue, 67.

7. For a full account of the development of the Arab Peace Initiative, see Marwan Muasher, *The Arab Center: The Promise of Moderation* (New Haven: Yale University Press, 2008), 102–33.

8. Conversation with a senior U.S. official in February 2011.

9. For a detailed discussion of Sharon's position and approach to peacemaking, see Muasher, *The Arab Center*, 192, 227–28.

10. The largest percentage (59 percent) believes that the *first* Palestin-

ian goal should be to end Israeli occupation in the areas occupied in 1967 and build a Palestinian state in the West Bank and the Gaza Strip, with East Jerusalem as its capital. See Palestinian Center for Policy and Survey Research, "Palestinian Public Opinion Poll No. (41)," September 27, 2011, http://www.pcpsr.org/survey/polls/2011/p41efull.html.

11. Including Moshe Arens, prominent leader of the Likud Party and a tough former Israeli minister of defense.

7.
Third Forces and the Battle for Pluralism

1. Max Weber, *Politics as Vocation* (Philadelphia: Fortress, 1965).

Index

Page numbers in italics refer to figures and tables.